lew Directions for
mmunity Colleges

Arthur M. Cohen
EDITOR-IN-CHIEF

Florence B. Brawer
ASSOCIATE EDITOR

Carrie B. Kisker
MANAGING EDITOR

Responding to the Challenges of Developmental Education

Carol A. Kozeracki
EDITOR

Number 129 • Spring 2005
Jossey-Bass
San Francisco

P9-EJH-449

RESPONDING TO THE CHALLENGES OF DEVELOPMENTAL EDUCATION
Carol A. Kozeracki (ed.)
New Directions for Community Colleges, no. 129

Arthur M. Cohen, Editor-in-Chief
Florence B. Brawer, Associate Editor

NEW DIRECTIONS FOR COMMUNITY COLLEGES (ISSN 0194-3081, electronic ISSN 1536-0733) is part of The Jossey-Bass Higher and Adult Education Series and is published quarterly by Wiley Subscription Services, Inc., A Wiley Company, at Jossey-Bass, 989 Market Street, San Francisco, California 94103-1741. Periodicals Postage Paid at San Francisco, California, and at additional mailing offices. POSTMASTER: Send address changes to New Directions for Community Colleges, Jossey-Bass, 989 Market Street, San Francisco, California 94103-1741.

SUBSCRIPTIONS cost $80.00 for individuals and $170.00 for institutions, agencies, and libraries. Prices subject to change. See order form in back of book.

EDITORIAL CORRESPONDENCE should be sent to the Editor-in-Chief, Arthur M. Cohen, at the Graduate School of Education and Information Studies, University of California, Box 951521, Los Angeles, California 90095-1521. All manuscripts receive anonymous reviews by external referees.

New Directions for Community Colleges is indexed in Current Index to Journals in Education (ERIC).

Microfilm copies of issues and articles are available in 16mm and 35mm, as well as microfiche in 105mm, through University Microfilms Inc., 300 North Zeeb Road, Ann Arbor, Michigan 48106-1346.

CONTENTS

EDITOR'S NOTES

The statistic is well-known: approximately four out of every ten entering community college students are found to be unprepared for college-level courses at their institutions, and as a result, enroll in one or more developmental classes (U.S. Department of Education, 1996, 2003). For some students, one semester in a precollege course is sufficient in order to progress to college-level courses; for others, developmental education becomes a curricular quicksand from which they do not emerge (Adelman, 1996; McCabe, 2000). In recent years a number of states have instituted policies that consolidate remediation at the community college, and in some cases, prohibit these programs from being offered in public four-year institutions (Healy, 1998; Jenkins and Boswell, 2002). These policies have created an unexpected confluence of the remedial and transfer missions of the community college, and have increased the pressure on community colleges to move students efficiently from developmental to college-level courses.

A number of influential scholars, most notably Boylan (2002) and Roueche and Roueche (1999), have conducted metanalyses of research on developmental education and have compiled a number of recommended instructional and organizational practices for developmental educators. Despite the availability of these models, community colleges—each of which faces its own unique combination of student needs and available resources—continue to struggle in their efforts to effectively educate underprepared students. This *New Directions for Community Colleges* volume explores the challenges of developmental education, presents research that evaluates existing programs, provides examples of effective practice, and suggests directions for future research.

Two main themes are woven throughout the chapters in this volume. The first is the danger posed by the isolation of developmental education: the frequent segregation of students into skill and drill classes devoid of academic content, the isolation of faculty whose many commitments, and often, part-time status, prohibit them from coming together to discuss ideas and approaches, and the separation of developmental courses from the broad array of support services that can enhance student learning. A strong case is made that the increased integration of these students, faculty, and programs into the broader academic structure of community colleges will result in improved outcomes for students. The second theme is the need for additional research to be conducted, especially systematic assessments of existing programs as well as qualitative research that captures the perceptions of students for whom these programs are designed.

In Chapter One, Jeanne Higbee, David Arendale, and Dana Lundell discuss the theoretical perspectives that influence the field of developmental education and present findings from current research, including studies on student perspectives and the efficacy of a wide array of developmental education models. They suggest that further research is needed in a number of areas, and call for researchers to take a holistic, qualitative approach to studying students' lives in determining how best to facilitate growth and development.

Chapter Two presents a statewide analysis of developmental education. Eric Bettinger and Bridget Terry Long discuss the characteristics and features of remedial education in Ohio community colleges, examine participation in the courses, and present findings on the effects of remediation on student decisions and outcomes. Their analysis goes a step further than much of the research in the field in that it compares differences in outcomes of similarly underprepared students enrolled in colleges with different assessment and placement policies.

In Chapter Three, Dolores Perin identifies the wide range of organizational and instructional approaches to developmental education that are in place in community colleges. She uses examples from a study of fifteen two-year colleges to introduce and illustrate a four-step decision-making template that college administrators and faculty can use to identify areas in their developmental education program that can be improved, to gather relevant information about student outcomes, and to identify and implement appropriate instructional and organizational changes.

Carol Kozeracki relates the findings from a study of three dozen developmental English instructors in Chapter Four. The chapter reveals the challenges that faculty face in teaching developmental courses, and discusses the roles played by graduate programs, college-based professional development programs, and professional associations in preparing faculty to meet the needs of their students.

Gillies Malnarich, in Chapter Five, begins with an overview of what it means to be "at risk" in higher education. She uses this as a starting point to discuss learning communities in relation to three complementary strands of research: key factors associated with educational completion, students' conceptions of their own abilities and the implications for persistence, and the effects of collaborative pedagogy on student engagement. This research informs the different learning community approaches that have been designed to turn student potential into measurable results.

Metropolitan Community College in Nebraska has created several learning communities for students at the developmental level. As described by Susan Raftery in Chapter Six, the AIM for Success program brings together student services personnel and faculty from different disciplines to address both the academic and nonacademic barriers faced by at-risk students. The success of this initiative has generated a collegewide discussion about interdisciplinary collaboration among faculty in a number of disciplines, and has inspired additional learning communities for different populations of students.

For decades, the City University of New York has been on the cutting edge of open admissions and educational access. In recent years, it has also been among the first higher education systems to limit developmental education to the community colleges. In Chapter Seven, Nancy Ritze describes how one of its institutions, Bronx Community College, has addressed the delicate balance between student access and support by devising a range of developmental education programs for a variety of student populations.

Hudson Valley Community College has taken a wide-ranging approach to addressing student underpreparedness by creating an Instructional Support Services and Retention unit that addresses the needs of all at-risk students. As Kathleen Quirk reports in Chapter Eight, the unit consolidates academic support services, which usually operate in isolation on a college campus, to reach students who may not be served by the traditional developmental program. With a centralized system and combined budget, program administrators are able to direct resources, both human and monetary, to student support services anywhere on campus.

In the final chapter, W. Norton Grubb and Rebecca Cox present a framework for assessing classroom effectiveness. They assert that there is a need to properly align pedagogy, student needs, curricular content, and institutional support in order to make educational programs, including developmental programs, more effective. They particularly emphasize the need for more research on students' attitudes toward learning and the ways in which students move from initial assessments, to developmental courses, to college-level and advanced classes. They conclude with a series of recommendations for colleges to consider in developing a coherent plan that aligns these four elements in the developmental education classroom.

Collectively, these authors offer a realistic assessment of the challenges faced by community colleges as they attempt to assist students who are similarly characterized as being underprepared for college-level work but whose academic preparation, motivational levels, goals, and needs are extraordinarily varied. They provide examples of successful programs and offer a number of recommendations that college administrators can adapt to their campuses and student populations in order to assist students as they move through developmental courses and toward their goals.

As a concluding remark, it is important to acknowledge that the choice of whether to use the term *developmental education* or *remedial education* continues to be controversial. Many people in the field have moved away from using the term *remedial*, because they believe it emphasizes students' deficiencies rather than their potential (Casazza, 1999). Others consider remedial courses to be a single component under the broader umbrella of developmental education (Boylan, Bonham, and Rodriguez, 2000). Ideally, using the term *developmental* instead of *remedial* reflects both a more sophisticated and informed approach to teaching and a different attitude about the students who enroll in these courses. However, some people worry that the latter term has simply been substituted for the former in an attempt to avoid the negative connotations associated with *remedial*. Both terms appear regularly in the literature; *developmental* is used more often by scholars in the field, but *remedial* is frequently used by policymakers and politicians. Throughout this volume, both terms are used in keeping with the preferred terminology of the authors and the research cited.

Carol A. Kozeracki
Editor

References

Adelman, C. "The Truth About Remedial Work." *Chronicle of Higher Education,* 1996, 43(6), A56.

Boylan, H. R. *What Works: Research-Based Best Practices in Developmental Education.* Boone, N.C.: Continuous Quality Improvement Network with the National Center for Developmental Education, 2002.

Boylan, H. R., Bonham, B. S., and Rodriguez, L. M. "What Are Remedial Courses and Do They Work: Results of National and Local Studies." *Learning Assistance Review,* 2000, 5(1), 5–14.

Casazza, M. E. "Who Are We and Where Did We Come From?" *Journal of Developmental Education,* 1999, 23(1), 2–7.

Healy, P. "CUNY's 4-Year Colleges Ordered to Phase Out Remedial Education." *Chronicle of Higher Education,* 1998, 44(39), A26.

Jenkins, D., and Boswell, K. *State Policies on Community College Remediation: Findings from a National Survey.* Denver: Education Commission of the States, Center for Community College Policy, 2002.

McCabe, R. H. *No One to Waste: A Report to Public Decision Makers and Community College Leaders.* Washington, D.C.: Community College Press, 2000.

U.S. Department of Education, National Center for Education Statistics. *Remedial Education at Higher Education Institutions in Fall 1995* (NCES 97–584). Washington, D.C.: U.S. Department of Education, 1996.

U.S. Department of Education, National Center for Education Statistics. *Remedial Education at Degree-Granting Postsecondary Institutions in Fall 2000. Statistical Analysis Report* (NCES 2004–010). Washington, D.C.: U.S. Department of Education, 2003.

Roueche, J. E., and Roueche, S. D. *High Stakes, High Performance: Making Remedial Education Work.* Washington, D.C.: Community College Press, 1999.

CAROL A. KOZERACKI is assistant director of the Institute for the Study of Educational Entrepreneurship at UCLA.

1

*This chapter summarizes theoretical perspectives
and research findings on developmental education, and
emphasizes the importance of considering students' voices
and experiences in determining how best to facilitate
growth and development in college.*

Using Theory and Research to Improve Access and Retention in Developmental Education

Jeanne L. Higbee, David R. Arendale, Dana Britt Lundell

Developmental education is an essential part of the community college mission; McCabe and Day (1998) estimate that more than two million students each year would drop out of postsecondary education without participation in one or more developmental education activities. To provide effective developmental education, community colleges should implement best practices that have been proven effective through rigorous research and evaluation based on strong theoretical foundations. This chapter discusses the primary theoretical perspectives that have shaped the profession and provide the foundation for today's professional practice, presents current research that reflects both student and institutional perspectives in evaluating a wide array of developmental education models, and concludes with recommendations for future research.

Theoretical Foundations of Developmental Education

Although most developmental educators are knowledgeable about the theories that guide their academic disciplines, many admit to lacking training in educational and related theories and do not perceive that there are many professional development opportunities to learn more about theory (Chung and Higbee, 2004). Thus, there is a critical need to link theory, research, and practice in developmental education.

Developmental education, previously known as *preparatory, compensatory,* or *remedial* education (Clowes, 1982). was renamed and redefined in order to encompass both the academic and noncognitive factors that influence student success in higher education. As Boylan and Saxon (1998) assert, developmental education not only focuses on enhancing students' academic performance but also takes into account "a variety of noncognitive or 'developmental' factors . . . [such] as locus of control, attitudes toward learning, self-concept, autonomy, ability to seek help, and a host of other influences having nothing to do with students' intellect or academic skill" (p. 7).

The roots of developmental education as practiced today can be traced to *The Student Personnel Point of View*, which proposed, "It is the task of colleges and universities to . . . assist the student in developing to the limits of his potentialities and in making his contribution to the betterment of society" (American Council on Education, 1937, as reprinted by National Association of Student Personnel Administrators, 1989, p. 39). *The Student Personnel Point of View* suggested that institutions of higher education promote the growth of "the student as a whole" (p. 39), rather than focusing merely on students' intellectual development. *The Student Personnel Point of View* was revised in 1949 (American Council on Education, 1949) to include a section on the need for academic assistance programs, and stated that it is the responsibility of colleges and universities to provide counseling and other services to assist students in developing the skills and attitudes necessary for success. Two theoretical frameworks—student development theory and transformative theory—echo the principles embodied in *The Student Personnel Point of View* and have strongly influenced developmental educators.

Student Development Theory. Arthur Chickering, William Perry, and Alexander Astin are three theorists whose work has guided developmental education since the 1960s. Chickering's (1969) model built on *The Student Personnel Point of View*'s emphasis on the whole student and identified seven vectors of college student development: achieving competence, managing emotions, developing autonomy, establishing identity, freeing interpersonal relationships, clarifying purpose, and developing integrity. Although there were relatively few nontraditional-age students enrolled in America's community colleges at the time Chickering developed his theory, many of the seven vectors also apply to older students who are developing new competencies and reexamining their sense of identity and purpose (Chickering and Reisser, 1993). Chickering's seven vectors can be particularly useful in identifying the competing demands on community college students' time and in demonstrating that development can occur simultaneously in many aspects of students' lives.

Perry's (1970) scheme of ethical and intellectual development is another student development theory that assists developmental educators in understanding student behavior. Perry argued that when students enter college, they are likely to view the world from a dualistic perspective and to look to faculty as authority figures who are there to provide the "right" answers. Following Perry's theory that educators must work to move students beyond this dualistic perspective, it is critical that community college developmental educators facilitate students' ability to think for themselves, evaluate the relative merits of different points of view, and make commitments accordingly.

Astin's (1984, 1985) theoretical work has also been a primary source of knowledge about college student development. He proposed that instead of viewing higher education as a place to produce "knowledge and trained manpower," educators must embrace a "talent development model," recognizing that where students begin along the educational continuum is not as important as how much they learn and develop (1985, pp. 14, 16). As he noted, "Under this model, the major purpose of any institution of higher education is to develop the talents of its faculty and students to their maximum potential. . . . The verb *develop* seems more appropriate than the verb *produce*" (1985, p. 16). Astin's work has encouraged educators to focus on a model that enhances access and retention and stresses the role of developmental education in nurturing students' individual talents. Although much of the research that served as the foundation for Chickering, Perry, and Astin's work was conducted at four-year institutions, these principles apply equally well to community colleges. As noted by Grubb and Worthen in their study of community colleges (1999), "Bridging the gap between the competencies students bring with them and those they need to do well in the classroom and in society is crucial to making them useful members of society" (p. 173).

Transformative Theories. Drawn from democratic theory, multicultural education theory, and other transformative perspectives, "Transformative education . . . places the student's reflective processes at the core of the learning experience and asks the student to evaluate both new information and the frames of reference through which the information acquires meaning" (American College Personnel Association and National Association of Student Personnel Administrators, 2004, p. 9). In the 1990s, postsecondary educators articulated a new emphasis on learning rather than teaching (Barr and Tagg, 1995), and developmental educators embraced this paradigm shift (Arendale, 1997). More recently, the American College Personnel Association and the National Association of Student Personnel Administrators (2004) asserted that "learning, as it has historically been understood, is included in a much larger context that requires consideration of what students know, who they are, what their values and behavior patterns are, and how they see themselves contributing to and participating in the world in which they live" (pp. 9–10). This message is particularly important to developmental educators working in community colleges, where attending classes is often but one of many commitments that students must balance. It is critical that developmental educators attend to the lived experiences of their students and focus on affective and cultural aspects of learning, not just on the cognitive domain.

Thus, it is not enough for developmental educators to be knowledgeable about the theories that guide their individual disciplines; they must also explore how individual students construct knowledge and interact with the institution, examine their own attitudes, and identify sources of inequities in higher education. By applying student development and transformative theories to their practice, developmental educators can have a long-term impact on access and retention while also establishing frameworks for conducting research about how students learn and develop.

Understanding Developmental Education Through Student Voices

Research on college students related to issues of access, learning support, retention, and preparation has gained momentum in recent decades. This research encompasses a broad range of issues, such as learning communities, attrition and retention, the impact of programmatic features on student performance, and student outcomes in developmental programs. Scholars have primarily taken a quantitative approach toward studying these areas; few have centrally featured student voices and the nature of their educational experiences.

Research that listens more directly to students' voices and perceptions of their own college experiences includes case studies, interviews, surveys, and focus groups. Developmental education can benefit greatly from this type of research, especially longitudinal studies that track students through their college transitions and explore changes in attitudes, beliefs, achievement, identity, and self-perceptions. In addition, by focusing on issues of access and preparation, researchers can provide information about possible barriers, motivational issues, diversity and cultural factors, and students' learning orientations. Future research that connects the characteristics of students in developmental programs with research on access and retention will help improve teaching and learning in community colleges.

In the past five years a number of articles have been published featuring developmental students' perspectives, and many used qualitative approaches to gathering data about students in developmental education courses and programs (Beach, Lundell, and Jung, 2002; Cole, Goetz, and Wilson, 2000; Valeri-Gold and others, 2001). These qualitative studies are extremely important, and their results have the potential to reshape community college practices. For example, an educator might know quantitatively how a student is performing in a course based on traditional measures such as grade point average, specific exam grades, and other achievement markers. However, when a student arrives underprepared for college or is underperforming in a first-year course, learning more about the nature of this student's experience, including the influence of cultural background or peer and family communities, may produce further insights into improving performance. Because students' experiences are richly layered and complex, researching underlying causes and perceptions through listening to student voices can strengthen the work of developmental educators.

It is also important to look at the results of research on student voices outside the field of developmental education. Key qualitative studies have examined college student development, workforce transitions, and multicultural issues, and these studies should be included as reference points for the future work of community colleges (see, for example, Baxter Magolda, 2001; Light, 2001).

Models of Developmental Education

A wide variety of developmental education models exist, and the effectiveness of each varies among both community colleges and their students. The diversity of these models is a result of different underlying learning theories, policies, funding formulas, student population characteristics, historical traditions, political decisions, and state and local stakeholder expectations (Boylan, 2002). Despite this diversity, developmental education programs can be broadly categorized into two groups: prerequisite acquisition models and concurrent acquisition models.

Prerequisite Acquisition Models. Many underprepared community college students must participate in prerequisite remedial or developmental courses before they can enroll in classes that carry credit toward a degree or certificate. Remedial courses in English and mathematics were designed to ameliorate knowledge and skill deficiencies for students entering college. Beginning in the 1860s, this medical model approach, which focused on a "remedy" or "cure" rather than a more holistic approach to students' intellectual development, identified certain students considered in need of "treatment" because they were "academically backward or less able" (Clowes, 1982, p. 8). These courses are often criticized because many assume that the focus is on academic content usually covered in middle school or early high school. In addition, remedial classes that are offered without additional coordinated academic support activities have mixed outcomes for students (Roueche and Roueche, 1999).

Developmental courses, in contrast to remedial courses, focus on student strengths and address both cognitive and affective development in order to provide skills that are needed for success both in college and in life. Typical developmental courses include introductory algebra, college textbook reading, strategic learning, and basic composition. The findings from research studies that examine the effectiveness of these courses are also mixed. Grubb and Associates (1999) suggested that high course withdrawal and failure rates may be related to student boredom with classes in which skill and drill activities that bear little relationship to credit-bearing courses predominate.

Concurrent Acquisition Models. These models allow students to enroll in developmental and credit-bearing courses simultaneously.

Concurrent acquisition models can be further divided into three types: adjunct learning experiences for targeted "high-risk" content courses; coordinated programs that require student participation in developmental activities outside of class; and developmental education models that are embedded, infused, or mainstreamed into a content course in order to provide academic support and enrichment.

Examples of the adjunct approach include learning assistance centers, supplemental instruction, and tutoring. Learning assistance centers, especially those that work closely with course instructors, can be very beneficial for students. However, because enrollment is voluntary, not all students will take advantage of them. Supplemental instruction is a model in which students voluntarily attend out-of-class study review sessions, facilitated by fellow students, which integrate content and study skills. Supplemental instruction is one of the most widely adopted adjunct developmental education models in postsecondary education, and many studies have demonstrated its effectiveness (Arendale, 2004). Tutoring can also be an effective adjunct model, although most studies show that outcomes are better when tutors are trained personnel (Boylan, Bliss, and Bonham, 1997; Maxwell, 1997). However, most of these studies lack comparison groups, so it is difficult to estimate the impact of tutoring. Although learning assistance centers, supplemental instruction, and tutoring can all be effective models for providing developmental education, a big disadvantage of all of these voluntary adjunct experiences is that students who lack help-seeking behaviors—often those most at risk for academic failure—may not choose to participate (Dembo and Seli, 2004).

Unlike adjunct models, coordinated developmental education models require students to participate in activities that occur outside of the targeted content class but are closely coordinated with what occurs inside. An example of a coordinated program is the linked or paired course model. Students concurrently enroll in two courses: a content course (for example, Introduction to Psychology) and a learning strategies course. Cognitive learning strategies are applied to assignments and reading requirements from the content course, thus providing the opportunity for immediate application and reinforcement of both content and basic skills. Several studies have shown this model to be extremely effective in educating developmental students (McCabe and Day, 1998; Tinto, 1997).

Another variation on the coordinated approach is to require all students to participate in additional discussion sessions that integrate both academic content and learning strategy practice. Faculty coordinate the curricula and supervise discussions, which are led by a trained student. This approach improves on adjunct developmental education models by ensuring that all students participate in the enrichment activities, especially those who are least likely to seek the opportunity on their own. Hundreds of colleges across the country have adopted these programs as research has shown them to support positive student outcomes (Arendale, 2004). Two extremely successful examples of required discussion session programs are the Emerging Scholars Program at the University of California, Berkeley (Treisman, 1986) and Peer-Led Team Learning at The City College of New York (Dreyfus, 2003).

In embedded, infused, or mainstreamed developmental education models, best practices are directly integrated by the primary course instructor into classroom learning experiences. The course curriculum and the classroom environment are transformed through simultaneous instruction in both academic content and learning strategies. This seamless integration provides enriched learning experiences for all students and eliminates the need for prerequisite or adjunct courses, thereby saving time and money for both students and the institution. Successful embedded or infused developmental education models are federated learning communities (Malnarich and Associates, 2003) and the University of Minnesota General College approach (Higbee, Lundell, and Arendale, forthcoming).

Recommendations for Future Research

Although numerous studies have shaped the practice of developmental education, there are a number of areas in which further research is necessary before definitive judgments can be made about its effectiveness. New areas of research have emerged in response to changing demographics and political realities, ongoing scholarship across educational levels, and improved research protocols and procedures.

Assess Affective Barriers to Student Achievement. Much of the assessment that occurs in developmental education programs is related to admissions, testing and placement, and student success rates. Further assessment is needed that takes into account the affective barriers to student achievement. In order to facilitate the academic success of all learners, developmental education programs should use multiple measures to explore students' motivation, academic autonomy, and potential sources of stress. Although many formal measures are available, developmental educators can also create their own assessment devices, such as questionnaires and protocols for interviews and focus groups. Educators can also gain valuable information by inviting students for informal, individual appointments early in the academic term.

Evaluate Program Effectiveness. In order for developmental education programs to remain viable. it is imperative that their effectiveness be evaluated. For example, research should be conducted to determine whether students who complete developmental education courses are successful in subsequent, related, credit-bearing courses. In addition, developmental educators might consider the following questions in order to assess their programs and services.

What are the essential elements and components of our institution's developmental education model? In order to create the most cost-effective and successful programs, educators need to understand which specific activities and components of developmental education are essential and which can be discarded. King, Morris, and Fitz-Gibbon (1987) argue that limiting evaluation solely to program outcomes only answers the question "Did it work?" and does not address the deeper question "What worked and what did not?" (p. 9). Research that focuses on the process of the intervention in addition to the final product can yield valuable information that can be used in program revision and improvement.

Why is it that all students who need developmental education do not participate in it and that all participants do not achieve positive outcomes? As community college students become more and more diverse, learning theories that are sensitive to individual differences become increasingly relevant, and even essential. Some students do not avail themselves of developmental opportunities for cultural reasons; some simply lack confidence or have not yet developed help-seeking behaviors. Research on elementary and secondary education has focused considerable attention on these two areas and can serve as a basis for further investigation with community college students.

How can developmental education best practices become integrated in first-year courses? An increasing number of educators believe that developmental education can provide richer and more productive learning experiences for all students and can teach essential lifelong skills needed on the job and for informed citizenship. Careful research is needed to understand how classroom instructors in varied academic disciplines can effectively and efficiently embed best practices into their courses while maintaining academic rigor.

Which developmental education practices are effective, both in cost and in practice? There is currently no central location where educators and scholars can access a wide collection of carefully researched and evaluated developmental education programs. Although the standards published by the Council for the Advancement of Standards and the National Association for Developmental Education (Clark-Thayer, 1995) are a positive start, a central database that contains examples of rigorously evaluated developmental education practices is needed.

Engage in Qualitative Research. Although many of the preceding research questions can be addressed using quantitative methods, qualitative research contributes important knowledge to complex issues of access and retention in developmental education. Interviews, focus groups, and classroom observations provide information about students' perceptions of their educational experiences that cannot be captured or defined through traditional quantitative measures. Qualitative research brings a more nuanced view of the complexity of students' lived experiences and complements the more generalizable data that are gained through quantitative measures.

There are three primary and highly significant benefits of using qualitative methods to assess developmental education. First, they can illuminate the multiple and shifting realities of students in transition. Second, they can decrease the stigma of developmental programs by demonstrating the richness and overlapping variety of both developmental and nondevelopmental students' experiences. Stigma results from a lack of knowledge about the real lives of students and the realities of developmental education, and qualitative research can help supply that knowledge. Third, qualitative methods allow educators to explore more meaningfully the complexity of students' multicultural issues in developmental programs. Qualitative research can transform the work of community college administrators, educators, and students, and can be very helpful in improving developmental education programs and services.

Many community college educators are already incorporating qualitative assessment methods into their programs' evaluations, and this work adds to the knowledge base that informs developmental education. This research approach faces some barriers, however, including a lack of acknowledgment or appreciation for the underlying value of this kind of data and the limited time educators have available to conduct longitudinal research. Despite these barriers, becoming familiar with research on college students can help practitioners understand the key issues students face as they persist and succeed in the community college. Finally, this research must be designed from a solid theoretical base to ensure its reliability, validity, and direct connection to ongoing research. Qualitative research that values students' direct experiences, and researchers who listen to students' voices, will continue to provide useful information to community college educators and administrators.

Conclusion

Knowledge of relevant theory and research is essential if educators are to implement best practices in community college developmental education. Recent efforts such as the Twin Cities Metropolitan Higher Education Consortium's Developmental Education Initiative (Lundell, Higbee, and Hipp, 2004) demonstrate how faculty and staff from community colleges and research universities can collaborate to strengthen learning and support for students across institutions. Students are also an excellent resource for learning about the real impact of developmental practices and programs. It is essential that their viewpoints be recognized and reflected in the future work of the field. Expanding the conversation about developmental models, engaging in more collaborative research on best practices, and sharing results widely can help ensure a brighter future for community college participants in developmental education

References

American College Personnel Association and National Association of Student Personnel Administrators. *Learning Reconsidered: A Campus-Wide Focus on the Student Experience.* Washington, D.C.: American College Personnel Association and National Association of Student Personnel Administrators. 2004.

American Council on Education. *The Student Personnel Point of View.* Washington, D.C.: American Council on Education, 1937.

American Council on Education. *The Student Personnel Point of View* (rev. ed.). Washington, D.C.: American Council on Education, 1949.

Arendale, D. "Leading the Paradigm Shift from Teaching to Learning." *National Association for Developmental Education Newsletter,* 1997, 20(3), 1.

Arendale, D. (ed.). "Postsecondary Peer Cooperative Learning Programs Annotated Bibliography," 2004. http://www.tc.umn.edu/~arend011/Peerbib03.pdf. Accessed June 24, 2004.

Astin, A. W. "Student Involvement: A Developmental Theory for Higher Education." *Journal of College Student Personnel,* 1984, 25, 297–308.

Astin, A. W. *Achieving Educational Excellence.* San Francisco: Jossey-Bass, 1985.

Barr, R., and Tagg, J. "From Teaching to Learning—A New Paradigm for Undergraduate Education." *Change Magazine,* 1995, 27(6), 12–26.

Baxter Magolda, M. B. *Making Their Own Way: Narratives for Transforming Higher Education to Promote Self-Development.* Sterling, Va.: Stylus, 2001.

Beach, R., Lundell, D. B., and Jung, H. J. "Developmental College Students' Negotiation of Social Practices Between Peer, Family, Workplace, and University Worlds." In D. B. Lundell and J. L. Higbee (eds.), *Exploring Urban Literacy and Developmental Education.* Minneapolis: Center for Research on Developmental Education and Urban Literacy, General College, University of Minnesota, 2002. http://www.gen.umn.edu/research/crdeul. Accessed Aug. 5, 2004.

Boylan, H. R. *What Works: Research-Based Best Practices in Developmental Education.* Boone, N.C.: Continuous Quality Improvement Network with the National Center for Developmental Education, 2002.

Boylan, H. R., Bliss, L., and Bonham, B. "Program Components and Their Relationship to Student Performance." *Journal of Developmental Education,* 1997, 20(3), 2–9.

Boylan, H. R., and Saxon, D. P. "The Origin, Scope, and Outcomes of Developmental Education in the 20th Century." In J. L. Higbee and P. L. Dwinell (eds.), *Developmental Education: Preparing Successful College Students.* Columbia: National Resource Center for the First Year Experience and Students in Transition, University of South Carolina, 1998.

Chickering, A. W. *Education and Identity.* San Francisco: Jossey-Bass, 1969.

Chickering, A. W., and Reisser, L. *Education and Identity* (2nd ed.). San Francisco: Jossey-Bass, 1993.

Chung, C. J., and Higbee, J. L. "Addressing the 'Theory Crisis' in Developmental Education: Ideas from Practitioners in the Field." Unpublished manuscript, University of Minnesota, Minneapolis, 2004.

Clark-Thayer, S. (ed.). *National Association for Developmental Education Self-Evaluation Guides: Models for Assessing Learning Assistance/Developmental Education Programs.* Clearwater, Fla.: H and H Publishing, 1995.

Clowes, D. A. "More Than a Definitional Problem: Remedial, Compensatory, and Developmental Education." *Journal of Developmental and Remedial Education,* 1982, 4(2), 8–10.

Cole, R. P., Goetz, E. T., and Wilson, V. "Epistemological Beliefs of Underprepared College Students." *Journal of College Reading and Learning,* 2000, 31(1), 60–72.

Dembo, M. H., and Seli, H. P. "Students' Resistance to Change in Learning Strategies Courses." *Journal of Developmental Education,* 2004, 27(3), 2–4, 6, 8, 10–11.

Dreyfus, A. E. (ed.). "Peer-Led Team Learning," 2003. http://www.pltl.org. Accessed Nov. 1, 2004.

Grubb, W. N., and Associates. *Honored but Invisible: An Inside Look at Community College Teaching.* New York: Routledge, 1999.

Grubb, W. N., and Worthen, H. "Remedial/Developmental Education: The Best and the Worst." In W. N. Grubb and Associates (eds.), *Honored but Invisible: An Inside Look at Community College Teaching.* New York: Routledge, 1999.

Higbee, J. L., Lundell, D. B., and Arendale, D. R. *Integrating Intellectual Growth, Multicultural Perspectives, and Student Development: The General College Model.* Minneapolis: Center for Research on Developmental Education and Urban Literacy, General College, University of Minnesota, forthcoming.

King, J. A., Morris, L. L., and Fitz-Gibbon, C. T. *How to Assess Program Implementation.* Thousand Oaks, Calif.: Sage, 1987.

Light, R. *Making the Most of College: Students Speak Their Minds.* Cambridge, Mass.: Harvard University Press, 2001.

Lundell, D. B., Higbee, J. L., and Hipp, S. *Metropolitan Higher Education Consortium Developmental Education Initiative: Meeting the Needs of Under-Served Students in the Twin Cities Metropolitan Area.* Minneapolis: Center for Research on Developmental Education and Urban Literacy, General College, University of Minnesota, 2004. http://www.gen.umn.edu/research/crdeul/consortium.htm. Accessed Nov. 19, 2004.

Malnarich, G., and Associates. *The Pedagogy of Possibilities: Developmental Education, College-Level Studies, and Learning Communities.* National Learning Communities Project Monograph Series. Olympia: The Evergreen State College, Washington Center for Improving the Quality of Undergraduate Education in cooperation with the American Association of Community Colleges, 2003.

Maxwell, M. *Improving Student Learning Skills.* San Francisco: Jossey-Bass, 1997.

McCabe, R., and Day, P. *Developmental Education: A Twenty-First Century Social and Economic Imperative.* Mission Viejo, Calif.: League for Innovation in the Community College, 1998.

National Association of Student Personnel Administrators. *Points of View.* Washington, D.C.: National Association of Student Personnel Administrators, 1989.

Perry, W. G. *Forms of Intellectual and Ethical Development in the College Years: A Scheme.* Austin, Tex.: Holt, Reinhart and Winston, 1970.

Roueche, J. E., and Roueche, S. D. *High Stakes, High Performance: Making Remedial Education Work.* Washington, D.C.: Community College Press, 1999.

Tinto, V. "Classroom as Communities: Exploring the Educational Character of Student Persistence." *Journal of Higher Education,* 1997, 68(6), 599–623.

Treisman, P. U. "A Study of the Mathematics Performance of Black Students at the University of California, Berkeley." *Dissertation Abstracts International,* 1986, 47(5), 1641.

Valeri-Gold, M., and others. "Examining College Developmental Learners' Reasons for Persisting in College: A Longitudinal Retention Study." *Research and Teaching in Developmental Education,* 2001, 17(2), 27–40.

JEANNE L. HIGBEE *is professor and senior adviser for research in the Center for Research on Developmental Education and Urban Literacy, General College, University of Minnesota.*

DAVID R. ARENDALE *is assistant professor and adviser for outreach in the Center for Research and Developmental Education and Urban Literacy, General College, University of Minnesota.*

DANA BRITT LUNDELL *is program director for the Center for Research on Developmental Education and Urban Literacy, General College, University of Minnesota.*

2

This chapter explores the characteristics and features of remedial education at community colleges, examines participation in these courses, and reviews findings on the effects of remediation on student decisions and outcomes.

Remediation at the Community College: Student Participation and Outcomes

Eric P. Bettinger, Bridget Terry Long

Community colleges play an important role in remediation; over 40 percent of first-year students at public two-year colleges take remedial courses (U.S. Department of Education, 2003). Furthermore, recent developments suggest that many states are moving toward concentrating all remediation in their community college systems. For example, in 1999 the City University of New York (CUNY) passed a resolution to phase out most remedial education at the system's four-year institutions and move it to the community colleges. Likewise, California encourages students to complete their remediation at a two-year college before entering the four-year system. Several other states, including Arizona, Florida, Montana, South Carolina, and Virginia, prohibit public four-year universities from offering remedial education.

Despite the growing numbers of underprepared students who enroll in remedial courses at community colleges each year, little is known about the causal effects of remediation on student outcomes. Most of the studies on the topic are descriptive and provide only simple comparisons between remediated and nonremediated students. For example, a 1996 national study suggests that freshmen enrolled in remedial classes are less likely to

The authors thank the members of the Ohio Board of Regents for their support during this research project. Rod Chu, Darrell Glenn, Robert Sheehan, and Andy Lechler provided invaluable help with the data. In addition, the Lumina Foundation provided crucial funding to aid in this research. Erin Riley, Cathy Wegmann, and Karen Singer Smith provided excellent research assistance.

persist into their second year than those not in such classes (U.S. Department of Education, 1996). However, because students placed in remediation are not as well prepared to begin with and have lower achievement scores than others, it is not clear whether such results reflect the effect of remediation or pre-existing differences between students. In another study, the Ohio Board of Regents (2001) found that almost 40 percent of remedial math students never take a subsequent math course, and those who do are less likely to succeed than nonremedial students. However, this study did not attempt to explain how and why these outcomes differ across students. After assessing the literature on remediation, the Ohio Board of Regents concluded, "There are no known benchmark indicators addressing the success rates of higher education's remediation efforts" (2001, p. 4).

This chapter examines the effect of remedial education on community college student outcomes. Using a unique, longitudinal data set that tracks nearly thirteen thousand students over five years, we explore the characteristics and features of remedial education at community colleges, examine participation in the courses, and review findings on the effects of remediation on student decisions and outcomes. By comparing students in remediation to similarly underprepared students not required to take the courses, we provide evidence of the causal impact of remediation on student outcomes. Ultimately, this chapter reflects on how community colleges attempt to assimilate underprepared students and prepare them for future college-level work.

Ohio Board of Regents Data

The data used in this analysis are from the Ohio Board of Regents (OBR). Since 1998, the OBR has collected comprehensive student-level enrollment data using application and transcript information from the state's public colleges. Moreover, students' scores on entrance exams, usually the ACT, are also linked to the database. The ACT and its accompanying student survey provide test score data as well as self-reported information on high school preparation and performance. In total, the data provide extensive information on each student's family background, high school preparation, postsecondary intentions, and progress through college. In this analysis, we focus on first-time freshmen who enrolled in one of nineteen public two-year colleges in Ohio in fall 1998 and track them until spring 2003 (that is, for five years). Two-year technical colleges were excluded because of their specialized curricula and the differences in the academic intents of their students. Because the data include the entire Ohio public higher education system, we are able to distinguish between students who withdrew from school altogether and those who transferred to other Ohio public colleges. Although we do not have information on students attending private or out-of-state colleges, data from the Integrated Postsecondary Education Data System indicate that these numbers are small and relatively insignificant.

The data set used in this chapter is specific to Ohio, yet it is expected to reflect patterns in other states and at the national level. Ohio has college enrollment and remediation rates similar to national patterns. Ohio high school graduates enter public higher education the following fall in percentages resembling the national averages: 69.6 percent of Ohio high school students graduate compared with the national average of 66.1, and 56.1 percent of Ohioans continue on to college compared with a national average of 56.7 percent (Mortenson, 2002). Furthermore, the percentage of Ohio students enrolling in remedial reading, writing, and math closely reflects the national averages. Thus, the data and results described in this chapter can be at least somewhat generalized to other states across the nation.

Organization and Delivery of Remedial Education

The purpose of remedial education is to provide underprepared students with the skills necessary to succeed in college and gain employment in the labor market. This practice has been around since the seventeenth century, when Harvard College assigned tutors to underprepared students studying Latin (Phipps, 1998). However, during the twentieth century, the increased demand for higher education among students from all backgrounds accelerated the need for remediation in higher education. By 1995, 81 percent of public four-year colleges and 100 percent of public two-year colleges offered remediation (U.S. Department of Education, 1996).

With the exception of Miami University and Central State University, all public colleges in Ohio offer remedial courses to entering freshmen. However, as in many states, most remedial students take their courses at community colleges, and roughly 55 percent of traditional-age, first-time freshmen in community colleges enroll in remedial courses (Ohio Board of Regents, 2001). In addition, half of Ohio's two-year colleges provide remedial or developmental courses to local business and industry (U.S. Department of Education, 1996).

There are two primary rationales for shifting remediation to the community colleges both in Ohio and nationwide. First, many administrators and faculty philosophically disagree with the practice of teaching precollege-level courses at four-year institutions; they feel that community colleges and high schools are more appropriate places to provide such instruction. Second, it is generally more costly to remediate a student at a four-year institution than at a two-year institution. For example, the average salary of a full-time faculty member at a public doctoral institution is almost $72,000, whereas the average salary of a full-time faculty member at a public two-year institution is about $51,000. This difference in salary—which is only a part of the overall cost of remediation—means that shifting courses to community colleges can result in substantial savings.

The cost has led some states to find other solutions to financing remediation. For example, Texas recently passed legislation that limits government funding of developmental coursework to a set number of credits, and legislators in states such as Tennessee and Utah have discussed banning the use of state money for remediation or asking students to pay for their remedial courses (Education Commission of the States, 2003). In addition, some state officials interpret the increasing role of remediation as a signal of high school ineffectiveness, and look to secondary school systems for funding. Several high school districts in Virginia have taken this so far as to *guarantee* their diplomas by paying the remedial expenses of their former students (Wheat, 1998). However, this type of action does not fully address the problem; only 64 percent of students taking remedial courses have earned a standard high school diploma, and many argue that high school graduation standards do not coincide with the competencies needed in college (McCabe, 2001).

Institutional remedial policies vary among community colleges. Often, however, remedial courses do not count toward degree or certification credits. Therefore, remediation frequently lengthens the time necessary to complete a degree, which can have implications for time-limited financial aid packages. Moreover, remedial courses are often the gateway for students to enroll in upper-level courses; about two-thirds of campuses across the nation restrict enrollment in some classes until remediation is complete (U.S. Department of Education, 1996). In Ohio, campuses vary in the extent to which they require underprepared students to enroll in remedial or developmental courses (Ohio Board of Regents, 2002). This practice may also influence the majors in which students can enroll; some majors offer little leeway for students to enroll in nonrequired and developmental classes. This, in turn, may affect students' ability to enter their chosen field or occupation.

Remedial Placement Processes

Although Ohio has statewide standards to distinguish between remedial and college-level work, community colleges frequently interpret these standards differently. At most community colleges, students take placement exams at the beginning of their freshman year. All Ohio community colleges use the Computerized Adaptive Placement Assessment and Support Systems (COMPASS) as a placement exam, and some also use the Assessment of Skills for Successful Entry and Transfer (ASSET); both exams are published by ACT, Inc. Placement tests consist of a variety of sections that measure students' skill levels in certain subject areas. For example, ASSET is a written exam with as many as twelve subsections that assess students' writing, numerical, and reading skills. Students are assigned to either remedial or college-level courses, depending on their scores. Usually, colleges make these designations based on hard cutoffs; students who score below a given threshold are assigned to remedial courses. These hard cutoffs may facilitate easier comparisons across universities; however, in Ohio, these data are not yet available from the various community colleges.

Participation in Remedial Education

This chapter focuses on traditional-age community college students in remedial programs: those who enter college within two years of high school graduation and are generally eighteen to twenty years old. These traditional-age students tend to be similar to older community college students in both race and gender; however, they are more likely to intend to complete a two- or four-year degree than older students. Furthermore, among these traditional-age students, those who seek a degree are more likely to be female and to have taken the ACT. In addition, the average ACT score for traditional-age remedial students is around 19; it is slightly higher among those seeking a degree.

In Ohio, almost 60 percent of traditional-age students at community colleges enroll in remedial math, and almost 40 percent enroll in remedial English. These overall numbers, however, mask the significant differences that exist in the characteristics of those students who participate in math and English remediation compared to those who do not. Although nearly 62 percent of women are placed in math remediation, only 54 percent of men place into these classes. Over three-fourths of black and Hispanic students are placed in math remediation courses, compared with 55 percent of whites. The difference is similarly large between the proportion of minority students (68 percent) and white students (39 percent) assigned to English remediation

Students who do not take the ACT are also more likely to be placed in remediation. As well, students who aspire to attain a degree are more likely to enroll in math remediation than non-degree-seeking students. In contrast, whether or not students aspire to a degree does not seem to affect enrollment in remedial English.

The need for remediation in college is closely tied to a student's course of study in high school. A 2002 study by the Ohio Board of Regents found that students who had completed an academic core curriculum in high school were half as likely to need remediation in college as students who had not completed a core. Hoyt and Sorensen (1999) found a similar pattern when examining the need for remediation at Utah Valley State College.

Our data reveal a similar story. Using a sample of students who took the ACT (and therefore had test score data and self-reported information on preparation), we found that students in math remediation reported lower high school GPAs in math, had taken fewer semesters of high school math, and scored lower on both the overall ACT and the math portion. Students enrolled in English remediation showed a similar pattern, as did the subset of ACT takers who indicated they aspired to a degree.

These findings suggest that underprepared students or those less successful in high school tend to be enrolled in remediation. However, it is important to note that previous studies found that many students who had successfully completed upper-level high school math courses still required remediation or needed to repeat subjects in college. In Ohio, 25 percent of those who completed a core high school curriculum still required remediation in either math or English (Ohio Board of Regents, 2002).

Remedial Course Completion

Even though a significant percentage of entering community college students are placed in remediation, many do not complete the courses. We found that approximately two-thirds of all Ohio community college students completed their first semester of remedial courses. However, female students were more likely to do so than their male counterparts, and younger students were more likely than their older peers to complete remediation. White and Asian students were also more likely to complete their courses than black or Hispanic students. Roughly 71 percent of remedial students who had taken the ACT completed remediation; only 56 percent of non-ACT takers did so. In addition, students who completed their remedial courses had higher ACT scores, more semesters of high school math and English, and higher high school GPAs in both math and English. Thus, age, race, and high school preparation are all significant predictors of completing remediation. Income, degree intent, and type of high school (public or private) generated differences in the likelihood of completing remediation, but were not statistically significant.

Effects of Remediation at Community Colleges

The effects of remediation are often evaluated by comparing students in remedial courses with those in college-level courses. Although these comparisons do not assess the causal effects of remediation, they can offer some basic insights into how outcomes differ for different types of students.

Table 2.1 presents outcomes of degree-seeking students who took the ACT by placement in remedial math. The results are broken down by full-time and part-time attendance, because the number of credits completed differs by attendance status. In general, students in remediation fared worse than their counterparts. Among full-time students, those in remediation completed 5.4 fewer credit hours on average than students not in remediation. They were also 15 percent more likely to have stopped out without a two-year degree, and 3.6 percent more likely to have stopped out without a four-year degree. They were also less likely to have transferred to a four-year college by spring 2003. Furthermore, by spring 2003, full-time students who were placed in remediation were almost 4 percent less likely to have completed a four-year degree within five years and 11 percent less likely to have completed a two-year degree. Among part-time students, those in remediation were less likely to complete two- or four-year degrees or transfer to a four-year school, but they completed more credit hours on average than nonremedial part-time students.

Table 2.1. Outcomes by Remedial Placement in Math

	Full-Time Students		Part-Time Students	
	Nonremedial	Remedial	Nonremedial	Remedial
Stopped out by spring 2003 without a two-year degree	62.46	77.46	83.13	89.28
Mean credit hours completed	45.83	40.42	28.71	30.84
Completed a two-year degree within five years	29.11	17.66	11.65	8.58
Transferred to a four-year college	23.18	18.90	14.26	12.45
At a four-year college as of spring 2003	7.42	4.25	4.26	1.37
Completed a four-year degree within five years	8.44	4.88	5.22	2.14
N	2,027	2,769	498	513

Note: Sample includes first-time, degree-seeking, traditional-age students who entered Ohio community colleges in fall 1998 and took the ACT. Numbers are percentages, except as otherwise indicated.

Outcomes for students in remedial English courses are illustrated in Table 2.2. Much like those in math remediation, both full-time and part-time students in remedial English completed fewer credit hours, and were less likely to have enrolled at a four-year college by spring 2003. In addition, full-time students in remedial English were 4.6 percent less likely to complete a four-year degree, and 9.2 percent less likely to complete a two-year degree than students not placed in remediation.

Although a simple comparison suggests that remedial placement has a negative impact on students, it masks the fact that students are not randomly placed in remediation. Better-prepared students are less likely to be placed in remediation and they also do better in college. Thus, simply comparing remedial students with nonremedial students is an unsatisfactory way to establish the true effects of remediation.

In order to examine the causal effects of remediation, we compared students with similar backgrounds and levels of academic preparedness at colleges with different remedial placement policies. The variation in cutoff scores for remedial placement allowed us to hold student backgrounds and amount of preparation constant while comparing student outcomes by whether or not they enrolled in remedial courses.

A more detailed explanation of the methods used in this regression analysis, including the ways we addressed endogeneity, can be found in Bettinger and Long (2004). In short, because students are more likely to attend colleges close to their home, we used distance to predict college attendance, and variation in remediation policies across colleges to predict the likelihood of remediation at any given institution. This methodology allowed us to compare outcomes of similar students who may have had different access to remediation.

Table 2.2. Outcomes by Remedial Placement in English

	Full-Time Students		Part-Time Students	
	Nonremedial	Remedial	Nonremedial	Remedial
Stopped out by spring 2003				
without a two-year degree	66.41	80.21	85.24	88.81
Mean credit hours completed	45.05	38.19	30.10	29.02
Completed a two-year degree				
within five years	25.64	16.43	10.48	9.09
Transferred to a four-year college	24.27	13.85	15.21	8.63
At a four-year college as of				
spring 2003	6.90	3.06	3.07	2.10
Completed a four-year degree				
within five years	7.95	3.36	4.28	2.10
N	3,159	1,637	725	286

Note: Sample includes first-time, degree-seeking, traditional-age students who entered Ohio community colleges in fall 1998 and took the ACT. Numbers are percentages, except as otherwise indicated.

Once differences in students' backgrounds are accounted for, remedial education no longer affects students negatively. Indeed, students who were placed in math remediation were found to be 15 percent more likely to transfer to a four-year college than students with similar test scores and high school preparation who attended colleges with policies that did not require placement in remedial courses. Moreover, students in math remediation took roughly ten more credit hours than their nonremedial counterparts. Participation in remedial math courses does not appear, however, to affect either the likelihood that students stop out or the likelihood that they complete a degree of any type. Outcomes for students placed into remedial English were not significantly different than those for nonremedial English students. Our English results, however, are much less precise than our math results because it is more difficult to control for variations in English remediation assignment across campuses than it is for math remediation assignment.

Conclusions

It is clear from these results that students in remediation do not perform worse than similar individuals who do not enroll in remedial courses. Simple comparisons of the two groups mask this effect by comparing dissimilar students. When we compare students with similar characteristics, we find that remediation does not appear to have a negative effect. In fact, math remediation appears to improve some student outcomes. These results are similar to other studies of remedial students at four-year colleges and universities (for example, Bettinger and Long, 2004). Despite these findings, community colleges must continue to find ways to improve remedial programs; even though our regression found that remediation does not have negative effects on students, one might have expected to find a greater number of positive effects.

It seems that community college remediation has both drawbacks and benefits. Certainly, not all students who place into remediation will choose to complete their courses. Perhaps placement into remediation sends a negative signal and suggests to students that they do not belong in college. In this way, remediation might serve to sort students in and out of higher education. However, other students will complete their remedial courses and have the same (or even better) chance of completing their degree objective as similar students who never enrol in remediation. As our results suggest, although community colleges will invariably lose some students because of remediation, they will help other students, particularly those enrolled in remedial math. In addition, the positive effects of remediation are likely to be larger among students who complete all of their remedial courses.

Thus our work suggests that remediation can have a positive overall effect on community college students, but there appears to be much room for improvement. For example, it is not clear that remediated students at community colleges fare better than similar students not required to take the classes. Moreover, the results for English remediation suggest no conclusive positive or negative impact on students. One way to improve the outcomes might be to implement programmatic and student support structures that can help increase the number of students who complete their remedial courses. However, additional research is needed to understand how institutional policies, student support structures, and other community college programmatic features can help increase the positive effects of remediation.

References

Bettinger, E. P., and Long, B. T. "Shape Up or Ship Out: The Effects of Remediation on Students at Four-Year Colleges" (Working Paper no. w10369). Cambridge, Mass.: National Bureau of Economic Research, 2004.

Education Commission of the States, Center for Community College Policy. *State Files.* Denver: Education Commission of the States, Center for Community College Policy, 2003. http://www.communitycollegepolicy.org/html/top.asp?page=/html/state_files _main.asp. Accessed Nov. 19, 2004.

Hoyt, J. E., and Sorensen, C. T. *Promoting Academic Standards?: The Link Between Remedial Education in College and Student Preparation in High School.* Orem: Utah Valley State College, Department of Institutional Research and Management Studies, 1999.

McCabe, R. H. "Developmental Education: A Policy Primer." *Leadership Abstracts,* 2001, 14(1), n.p. http://www.league.org/publication/abstracts/leadership/labs0201.htm. Accessed Nov. 22, 2004.

Mortenson, T. "Chance for College by Age 19 by State in 2000." *Postsecondary Education Opportunity,* 2002, *123,* n.p.

Ohio Board of Regents. *Ohio Colleges and Universities 2001. Profile of Student Outcomes, Experiences and Campus Measures.* Columbus: Ohio Board of Regents, 2001.

Ohio Board of Regents. *Making the Transition from High School to College in Ohio 2002.* Columbus: Ohio Board of Regents, 2002.

Phipps, R. *College Remediation: What It Is, What It Costs, What's at Stake.* Washington, D.C.: Institute for Higher Education Policy, 1998. http://www.ihep.com/Pubs/PDF/ Remediation.pdf. Accessed Aug. 16, 2004.

U.S. Department of Education, National Center for Education Statistics. *Remedial Education at Higher Education Institutions in Fall 1995* (NCES 97–584). Washington, D.C.: U.S. Department of Education, 1996.

U.S. Department of Education, National Center for Education Statistics. *Remedial Education at Degree-Granting Postsecondary Institutions in Fall 2000: Statistical Analysis Report* (NCES 2004–010). Washington, D.C.: U.S. Department of Education, 2003.

Wheat, I. D., Jr. *Deficient Diplomas: Is it Time for a Graduate Warranty Program?* Springfield, Va.: Thomas Jefferson Institute for Public Policy, 1998. http://www. thomasjeffersoninst.org/pdf/articles/deficient_diplomas.pdf. Accessed Jan. 18, 2005.

ERIC P. BETTINGER *is assistant professor of economics at the Weatherhead School of Management at Case Western Reserve University.*

BRIDGET TERRY LONG *is associate professor of economics at the Harvard Graduate School of Education.*

3

This chapter identifies current organizational and instructional approaches to developmental education in community colleges and recommends a process by which colleges can make institutionally appropriate decisions to improve developmental education outcomes.

Institutional Decision Making for Increasing Academic Preparedness in Community Colleges

Dolores Perin

The teaching of precollege reading, writing, and math became a necessity in community colleges by the early 1970s, as their doors began to open to all students, whatever their level of academic preparedness (Dougherty, 1994). Across the country, community colleges created developmental education programs to provide basic academic skills instruction, counseling, and other support to academically underprepared students. Today, these programs are a prominent feature of community colleges, and without them postsecondary access would be seriously curtailed.

However, despite the importance of developmental education, there are differing claims as to its effectiveness. Further, it is not clear how these programs should be organized within colleges, and there are many accounts of innovations being tried in individual developmental education classrooms as instructors struggle to identify effective teaching methods. Issues of effectiveness, organization, and instruction suggest that optimal models of developmental education remain to be identified. Finally, the community college population continues to diversify, with increasing numbers of students of racial, ethnic, and linguistic minorities and low socioeconomic status, more students who are the first in their families to attend college, and more who

The research described in this chapter was supported by funding from the Alfred P. Sloan Foundation to the Community College Research Center, Teachers College, Columbia University.

are considerably older than traditional college age. In response to the changing demographics, nontraditional approaches to education are increasingly needed. In this climate, community colleges are seeking ways to improve their developmental education programs.

The purpose of this chapter is to provide an overview of current organizational and instructional approaches to developmental education and recommend a process by which community colleges can make institutionally appropriate decisions to improve developmental education outcomes. Throughout this chapter the terms *developmental education* and *remediation* are used interchangeably, although they may reflect different philosophies.

Current Approaches to Developmental Education

Ideally, educational institutions should be able to base instruction and services on systemic evaluation data that point clearly to the benefits of one approach over another. However, such studies have not been conducted in most community college developmental education programs, and colleges cannot wait for controlled studies before they make decisions about how to promote the educational achievement of academically underprepared students. Pending such studies, they can consider adopting practices that other institutions have found promising.

The Community College Research Center recently conducted an in-depth case study with fifteen community colleges across the country (Perin and Charron, forthcoming) that identified a range of promising practices in developmental education. Information from interviews with instructors, administrators, and counselors, examination of instructional material, and classroom observations indicated that a great deal of innovation was in progress. However, the wide variety of organizational and instructional approaches at the colleges studied suggested a lack of consensus on ways to ready academically underprepared students for the college curriculum.

Organization of Developmental Education. Given the necessity of developmental education programs, community colleges need to decide whether to house them in stand-alone departments (centralized organization) or integrate them into regular academic departments (mainstreamed organization) (Perin, 2002; Shults, 2000). Centralization has been recommended in previous literature on the grounds that it makes it more likely that faculty will have a primary interest in teaching basic precollege academic skills, and because counseling and ancillary tutoring are more readily available (Boylan, Bliss, and Bonham, 1997; McCabe, 2003; Roueche and Roueche, 1999). Despite claims about the superiority of centralization, McCabe (2003) reports that most community colleges mainstream their developmental education programs.

This trend was also found in Perin and Charron's (forthcoming) study, where twelve of the fifteen colleges mainstreamed their developmental programs, one centralized them, and two used a mixed model. Among the twelve colleges with mainstreamed programs, five used "partial" main-streaming whereby the developmental education courses were housed in regular academic departments but coordinated separately. In the mixed models, different remedial areas were mainstreamed and centralized. For example, developmental writing and math courses could be taught in regular English and math departments, but developmental reading was provided through a separate department.

At one college, in addition to partial mainstreaming, a diffusion model was used, in which developmental courses were operated by one department and practice labs by another, creating difficulties in staff communication. In another example, self-paced, computer-assisted developmental education courses were taught in five different learning centers. A reading professor oversaw the delivery of reading instruction in these centers and reported to different senior administrators on curricular and delivery issues. Another college found it difficult to control the organization of developmental education because "little study centers" were sprouting up around campus despite an intention to centralize.

Although the ease of administering centralized and mainstreamed models seemed roughly the same, interviewees noted advantages and disadvantages of each model. Mainstreamed approaches benefited from economies of scale but did not prioritize the hiring of instructors with specialized backgrounds. For example, in a college where developmental education was mainstreamed, an instructor who had remedial expertise thought that it would be better to centralize the remedial courses, saying "We [developmental educators] don't believe English teachers can teach reading. Reading is a very specialized skill, and to help a disabled reader, you have to know a lot of things about what goes on in the brain to bring them forward." Instructors whose own academic backgrounds predispose them to teach literature and college math may not feel equipped or inclined to teach remedial students.

However, isolating remediation in a centralized structure may limit remedial instructors' awareness of the content and expected performance of the college-credit courses for which they intend to prepare students (Perin, 2002), and it may also reduce college-credit instructors' understanding of students' needs. Communication between regular and developmental education faculty may be limited in a centralized model, although college size might mediate this effect. At one of the smaller colleges in the sample, which followed a centralized model, frequent interactions between developmental education and college-credit instructors permitted regular communication about the needs of underprepared students.

Other factors that may affect the choice of organizational structure are remedial placement policy, size of academic department, and institutional politics. All of these concerns were seen at a case study site where developmental education was mandated for underprepared students and a centralized remedial department had been abolished because it was perceived by senior administrators to be too large and powerful. Colleges in which significant proportions of students are underprepared may prefer to distribute students across departments so that the whole college shares responsibility for the development of their knowledge and skills.

Despite the wide variety of organizational practices, Perin and Charron (forthcoming) found that many faculty thought centralization was most beneficial to students. Whichever model turns out to be the most effective, the lack of uniformity across community colleges suggests that the organization of developmental education is an ongoing institutional concern. The various issues described in the research literature make it difficult to recommend one model over another; the characteristics, policies, and goals of individual colleges need to be considered as organizational decisions are made.

Assessment and Placement. Most community colleges assess the academic skills of incoming students (Shults, 2000; U.S. Department of Education, 2003), but institutions vary in whether they require low-skilled students to enroll in developmental education (Perin, forthcoming). Some states, such as Texas, Illinois, and Florida, mandate remedial placement but leave specific decisions on how this is to be done to local institutions. As with the organization of developmental education, placement policy is highly variable across institutions, possibly because of a lack of consensus on the characteristics of college-level performance (Merisotis and Phipps, 2000; Oudenhoven, 2002; Phipps, 1998).

An interesting phenomenon found by Perin (forthcoming) is that both states and colleges may soften their own placement mandates by permitting the use of subjective assessment procedures, allowing the override of test scores, lowering cutoff scores, and substituting college-credit courses for remedial courses. At one college in the Perin and Charron (forthcoming) study, low-skilled students were exempt from remedial courses if they signed a waiver. In another, only one area of remediation was required, even if the student placed low in reading, writing, and math—with the stipulation that if math were selected, the student would have to complete the whole remedial math sequence. Another college in the sample mandated developmental education but permitted low-scoring students to take selected college-credit classes instead of skills classes because it did not have enough developmental sections. These policy adaptations may benefit both students and the institution, by facilitating access to the college curriculum for students who are eager to earn degrees, and by helping institutions respond to the threat of lowered enrollments. Thus, while colleges recognize the value of universal assessment, their actions often reflect the real-world challenges of mandatory placement.

New Course Formats. Traditionally, community colleges offer between two and four levels of developmental reading, writing, and math courses, which each run for one semester. At some colleges, the number of levels has been reduced in an attempt to speed up the completion of remediation and entry into the college-level curriculum. This reduction may result in increased retention and associated college access, but it may also result in a lowering of course standards because of the presence of underprepared students. Generally, administrators and students prefer fewer developmental course levels whereas instructors argue for more.

The standard course format includes several classroom sessions per week and an additional lab component providing tutoring and computer-based practice (Boylan, 2002). Often, developmental education enrollments are capped at lower levels than college-credit courses (McCusker, 1999). Most developmental courses bear institutional credit but do not count toward degrees.

By definition, the traditional approach predominates, but Perin and Charron (forthcoming) found a number of new course formats designed to increase student achievement, including self-paced, tutor-based, online, accelerated, intensive summer, contextualized, personalized, combined reading-writing, combined remedial and college English, study skills, off-site, alternation of instruction and application, and instruction following a quarterly rather than semester schedule.

Many of these new course formats are popular among developmental students. For example, when one of the colleges offered remedial math students a choice between a standard course and an open-entry, open-exit, self-paced course in a specialized math lab, two-thirds opted for the nontraditional format. At another institution, all developmental math was taught using self-paced and small-group work in class, and supplemented by tutoring during lab hours. Students were permitted take a state test for exit from remediation when they felt ready to pass. Previous literature indicates the need to prepare students to monitor, evaluate, and regulate their learning processes if a self-directed learning format is to succeed (Garrison, 1997).

A tutor-based remediation option was available at another college in the study for students who scored within ten points of passing the state placement exam. The option was so appealing to students that three full-time professional staff who were designated as tutors could not meet the demand (642 students in one semester). The tutoring was popular because it meant that students would not have to register for yet another remedial course and could receive instruction based directly on their individual skill patterns. If colleges have sufficient resources to hire experienced, professional tutors, this approach appears to be promising for helping students clear the last hurdle to exit from remediation.

Five of the colleges in the sample provided accelerated remedial courses. At one institution, students had a choice between half-semester and full-semester remedial reading courses. At another, a separately coordinated, five-week remedial math and writing program was offered to hasten students' preparation for the college curriculum. Short-term summer remedial courses were another example of accelerated remedial instruction; some of these were intended for students who had failed a remedial course during the academic year. Although the idea of accelerating developmental education seemed popular, there was also some resistance. At one college, administrators were reluctant to implement a district request for a fifteen-week fast track course (reduced from eighteen weeks) after experiencing difficulty finding classroom space. At another, instructors doubted the feasibility of acceleration because of the seriousness of students' academic difficulties. Although the institutions did not have outcomes data on these options, interviews revealed that although acceleration increases access to the college curriculum and might stem dropout, the process may leave some skills untaught, which may in turn threaten the quality of the college-credit courses, and ultimately, the long-term educational outcomes of low-skilled students.

Another modification of traditional developmental education was contextualized instruction, in which basic skills were linked to credit-bearing, disciplinary courses. For example, one remedial writing course taught nursing aspirants the writing skills they would need to produce documentation for the health care profession. Another new format was to combine reading and writing instruction, traditionally taught separately in community college developmental education. In another approach, one of the institutions offered a modified remedial course combining college-credit and developmental English. This was a six-hour offering for students with borderline scores on the writing portion of the placement test. Students could retake the test twice during the semester, and if they passed, continue with and receive credit for college-level English. All in all, the new formats represent attempts to improve outcomes for developmental education students. Institutions considering such changes would benefit from collecting systematic data to measure the effectiveness of these promising practices.

Instructional Improvement. Developmental education instruction has tended to focus on isolated skills (Grubb and Associates, 1999) but, in surveying recent developmental education literature, Perin and Charron (forthcoming) uncovered active searches for instructional improvement. These searches included the following classroom practices: providing explicit, structured, sequential instruction and prompt feedback; presenting information in small chunks, related to information students already have; using mastery learning and learner-centered, meaning-based instruction; linking basic skills to content applications; varying teaching approaches based on cognitive theory; using computers, electronic communication, and Web access; teaching for independent learning; incorporating student identity issues in teaching; promoting student-faculty contact and cooperation among students; accommodating different learning styles and abilities; aligning developmental education with college and state standards; hiring instructors who are credentialed, experienced in special education, and sympathetic to the needs of at-risk students; providing professional development; and assessing program achievements.

Most developmental educators would agree that some if not all of these strategies are useful; what is lacking is systematic, controlled evaluation that can inform institutional decision making.

In addition to numerous teaching methods that can be used to improve students' skills, connecting remedial courses with other courses through learning communities is a promising approach. Perin and Charron (forthcoming) found two kinds of learning communities involving remedial courses. One type clustered developmental courses for single cohorts of students, and the other linked remedial courses with one or more credit-bearing content courses. Learning communities that included developmental education courses were rare, however, possibly because many remedial courses are prerequisites for credit-bearing courses, or because of scheduling difficulties. Despite these barriers, positive outcomes have been reported for learning communities (Boylan, 2002; Tinto, 1997), which suggests that this innovation may be worth the considerable resources and effort needed for implementation in developmental education. Like other contextualized learning approaches, learning communities may help students generalize the skills learned in remedial courses to the content courses needed to earn a degree.

A Template for Effective Institutional Decision Making

The following section offers a four-step decision-making template to assist community college administrators and faculty who want to improve developmental education outcomes in their institutions. The steps, preliminary actions, and decisions presented here can be seen as a menu of options from which educators can choose, and can be modified and expanded as needed. There is no one way to improve developmental education, and all new practices must be consistent with institutional culture and goals.

Step 1: Gather Data. The first step in moving toward effective institutional decision making to improve developmental education is to identify available institutional data that can be used to understand outcomes of developmental education students. Examples include retention and pass rates in individual courses, exit rates from developmental education, semester-to-semester persistence rates, enrollment in higher-level courses, test scores and grades, and college graduation rates. Colleges without institutional research offices may be able to obtain relevant data from state databases or ask district or state offices to help them gather data on a regular basis.

Once the appropriate variables have been identified, colleges may decide to compare their developmental education outcomes with findings from peer colleges in the district or state. District or state standards will indicate the specific bases on which the effectiveness of new policies will be measured, and can help stakeholders focus on the need to evaluate the policy adjustments and innovations.

Step 2: Determine Outcomes. Once data have been collected, analysis of the evidence will allow the faculty and administrators to decide whether the information gathered permits meaningful conclusions about the performance of developmental education students in the institution.

Colleges might generate a list of specific questions in response to the evidence, including: Which skill areas and sections show the highest retention and pass rates? Do developmental education students in learning communities show better retention and pass rates than students with the same entering skills and demographics who are not in learning communities? What are the characteristics of instructors whose sections show better outcomes? What instructional methods are used in sections that show higher retention and pass rates? In institutions where remediation is voluntary, questions could be asked about the age, previous educational achievement, and goals of students who do and do not opt for developmental education courses.

After generating a list of questions, institutions should specify any additional data that need to be gathered, and can decide whether the measures, such as placement tests, are adequate and provide an accurate reflection of students' academic preparedness. If developmental student performance indicates that improvement is desired, the following steps can be taken.

Step 3: Identify Organizational and Instructional Options to Improve Outcomes. The third step in this template is to select at least one area that the institution can address to improve outcomes. The following list of options is not exhaustive, nor are all items applicable to all institutions. In each of the following areas, an example from previous research (Perin, 2001; Perin and Charron, forthcoming) is provided to indicate the complexity of changing existing remedial practice.

Organization of Developmental Education. To improve developmental education, colleges might change their current structure (centralized, fully or partially mainstreamed, or mixed) or work to improve the efficiency of the current organizational structure. They need to estimate the impact of the new organization on students, faculty, and the college in general, and create a procedure to evaluate and assess change in organizational structure. For example, if a college is too large to permit routine, informal interdepartmental communication, incentives could be provided for developmental and college-level instructors to collaborate formally to align their respective curricula. Procedures for reorganizing developmental education and promoting faculty collaboration could be designed by a panel of developmental and college-level instructors and administrators. However, resources must be made available to ensure faculty collaboration. In addition, instructor surveys and analyses of student retention and grade data should be used to indicate the results of the new organizational structure.

Assessment and Placement. Colleges might change their assessment instruments or cutoff scores for assignment into remedial courses if students are not succeeding at expected rates in college-level courses. They might also increase or decrease the number of remedial prerequisites for college-level courses. As part of this process the college must also estimate the impact that tightening or loosening the placement mandate would have on enrollment in and quality of college-level courses.

For example, if a college mandates developmental education but applies a low cutoff score on the initial placement test, many students may test out of remediation but not pass the college-level courses. In this case the college could raise the cutoff score, but it would need to allocate additional resources to fund a greater number of remedial sections. Further, the college would need to face the possibility that increased remedial placement could result in greater attrition and thus lowered enrollments. If this is unpalatable, the college may decide not to adjust the cutoff score and instead consider how to provide systematic instruction of basic academic skills to students as needed in college-level courses.

Instructional Format. To improve developmental instruction format, colleges might change the number of levels in one or more areas (reading, writing, math), add or reduce time in lab practice, or change the nature of lab practice. As well, colleges might create learning communities and make the necessary changes in registration procedures and program requirements to ensure adequate enrollment. Colleges might also accelerate or lengthen the time students spend in remediation or implement a new instructional format, such as self-paced, tutor-based, online, accelerated, intensive summer, contextualized, personalized, combined reading-writing, or combined remedial and college-level English. Finally, a college might incorporate study skills, off-site instruction, alternating instruction and application, or instruction following a quarterly rather than semester schedule.

One way to alter instructional format is to create learning communities, such as a cluster of courses for prenursing students that includes advanced developmental writing, introductory biology, and philosophy. Any content course can be selected, provided there are no prerequisites for remedial writing. To ensure adequate registration, the college can block prenursing students from registering for biology or philosophy sections that are not part of the learning community. As with all learning communities, it is most effective for the instructors of the three courses to collaborate and align their curricula rather than teach without reference to the others.

Instructional Strategies. Colleges can identify areas in which one or more new teaching strategies would be effective and appropriate for the levels at which they should be employed and for the instructors who employ them. For example, in institutions that enroll many recent high school graduates, instructional strategies that use electronic media, active projects, and immediate application to situations that the students see as meaningful may be more effective than instruction in isolated skills.

Step 4: Prioritize and Implement Organizational and Instructional Decisions. Once institutionally appropriate options for improving developmental education have been identified, colleges should prioritize institutional decisions, select those that are most pressing and feasible, and create a process for implementing them. Examples of implementation processes include faculty-administration collaboration, cross-disciplinary instructor collaboration, faculty development initiatives, and an institutional incentive system to promote change.

Previous research suggests that developmental education is changed more effectively when faculty are involved in creating the initial vision and designing the implementation procedures than when the change is presented from the top down. The instructors who are key to institutional change will be more likely to implement important classroom modifications if they collaborate with the administration throughout the decision-making process. Included in this collaboration should be the determination of how developmental education can be assessed and monitored on an ongoing basis to gauge the effects of institutional and instructional change.

Besides faculty-administrator collaboration, instructor partnerships set up to align remedial and content curricula can improve developmental education. Challenges for faculty collaboration include finding time for regular meetings and resolving disagreements that may arise in evaluation standards, reading selections, or in other areas. Cross-disciplinary faculty collaboration can be initiated and monitored through professional development activities, which should be given high visibility in the institution. Institutions might offer incentives to instructors to implement change. These incentives include summer pay, course release, awards, and opportunities for presentation and travel to national conferences.

Conclusions

This chapter uses a focused case study of fifteen community colleges and other relevant research to identify organizational and instructional approaches to developmental education currently employed at community colleges. This information can alert instructors and administrators to approaches that have been developed in recent years to improve the retention and performance of academically underprepared students.

This chapter also provides a template to guide colleges in making institutionally appropriate decisions to improve developmental education. The template does not identify a single best-practice approach but instead provides a process for community college faculty and administrators to follow in thinking about how to improve developmental student outcomes.

Because "research topics valued by individuals associated with universities may be quite distinct from research topics centered on contemporary community college issues" (Bers and Calhoun, 2002, p. 10), the template may not include items that are important in local institutions or may inappropriately overemphasize others. Optimally, users can adapt the template's components to address specific institutional goals. The template can help institutions prioritize goals that may ostensibly conflict with each other—for example, increasing access while simultaneously maintaining standards (Perin, forthcoming) or increasing baccalaureate transfer rates while keeping a commitment to educate underprepared students (Shaw and London, 2001).

In its current form the template addresses assessment, placement, instructional formats, and teaching strategies. It could be expanded, however, to incorporate other important areas, such as new student orientation, advising, English as a Second Language instruction, disability services, and the use of academic learning centers.

Although there are ample reports of best practices in existing literature (Boylan, Bliss, and Bonham, 1997; McCabe and Day, 1998; Roueche, Ely, and Roueche, 2001), few practices have been systematically evaluated. Lacking such studies, firm recommendations for changes in developmental education policy and instruction are premature. However, pending systematic evaluation evidence, community colleges can benefit from tracking their own initiatives using routinely collected institutional data. However, many colleges have not allocated the resources necessary to analyze data they have collected on the performance of developmental education students. Institutional use of the template offered in this chapter may encourage colleges to increase their use of student data.

Finally, it is important to acknowledge the difficulty of institutional change. As experienced practitioners already know, vision, risk taking, time, effort, and practical resources are necessary to effect the deep changes needed to boost the achievement of an increasingly diverse student body. Whether institutions approach change sequentially or reform several aspects of policy and instruction simultaneously, taking a close look at current practice and student data, in combination with the energetic collaboration of administrators and instructors, seems to offer promising approaches to improving developmental education and student achievement.

References

Bers, T. H., and Calhoun, H. D. "Literature on Community Colleges: An Overview." In T. H. Bers and H. D. Calhoun (eds.), *Next Steps for the Community College*. New Directions for Community Colleges, no. 117. San Francisco: Jossey-Bass, 2002.

Boylan, H. R. *What Works: Research-Based Best Practices in Developmental Education.* Boone, N.C.: Continuous Quality Improvement Network with the National Center for Developmental Education, 2002.

Boylan, H., Bliss, L., and Bonham, B. "Program Components and Their Relationship to Student Performance." *Journal of Developmental Education*, 1997, 20(3), 2–9.

Dougherty, K. *The Contradictory College: The Conflicting Origins, Impacts, and Futures of the Community College.* Albany: State University of New York Press, 1994.

Garrison, D. R. "Self-Directed Learning: Toward a Comprehensive Model." *Adult Education Quarterly*, 1997, 48(1), 18–34.

Grubb, W. N., and Associates. *Honored but Invisible: An Inside Look at Teaching in Community Colleges.* New York: Routledge, 1999.

McCabe, R. H. *Yes We Can! A Community College Guide for Developing America's Underprepared.* Phoenix, Ariz.: League for Innovation in the Community College and American Association of Community Colleges, 2003.

McCabe, R. H., and Day, P. R., Jr. (eds.). *Developmental Education: A Twenty-First Century Social and Economic Imperative.* Mission Viejo, Calif.: League for Innovation in the Community College, 1998.

McCusker, M. "ERIC Review: Effective Elements of Developmental Reading and Writing Programs." *Community College Review,* 1999, 27(2), 93–105.

Merisotis, J. P., and Phipps, R. A. "Remediation Education in Colleges and Universities: What's Really Going On?" *Review of Higher Education,* 2000, 24(1), 67–85.

Oudenhoven, B. "Remediation at the Community College: Pressing Issues, Uncertain Solutions." In T. H. Bers and H. D. Calhoun (eds.), *Next Steps for the Community College.* New Directions for Community Colleges, no. 117. San Francisco: Jossey-Bass, 2002.

Perin, D. "Academic-Occupational Integration as a Reform Strategy for the Community College: Classroom Perspectives." *Teachers College Record,* 2001, 103(2), 303–335.

Perin, D. "The Location of Developmental Education in Community Colleges: A Discussion of the Merits of Mainstreaming vs. Centralization." *Community College Review,* 2002, 30(1), 27–44.

Perin, D. "Can Community Colleges Protect Both Access and Standards? The Problem of Remediation." *Teachers College Record,* forthcoming.

Perin, D., and Charron, K. "Lights Just Click On Every Day: Academic Preparedness and Remediation in Community Colleges." In T. R. Bailey and V. S. Morest (eds.), *Defending the Community College Equity Agenda,* forthcoming.

Phipps, R. *College Remediation: What It Is, What It Costs, What's at Stake.* Washington, D.C.: Institute for Higher Education Policy, 1998.

Roueche, J. E., Ely, E. E., and Roueche, S. D. *In Pursuit of Excellence: The Community College of Denver.* Washington, D.C.: Community College Press, 2001.

Roueche, J. E., and Roueche, S. D. *High Stakes, High Performance: Making Remedial Education Work.* Washington, D.C.: Community College Press, 1999.

Shaw, K. M., and London, H. B. "Culture and Ideology in Keeping Transfer Commitment: Three Community Colleges." *Review of Higher Education,* 2001, 25(1), 91–114.

Shults, C. *Institutional Policies and Practices in Remedial Education: A National Study of Community Colleges.* Washington, D.C.: American Association of Community Colleges, 2000.

Tinto, V. "Classrooms as Communities: Exploring the Educational Character of Student Persistence." *Journal of Higher Education,* 1997, 68(6), 599–623.

U.S. Department of Education, National Center for Education Statistics. *Remedial Education at Degree-Granting Postsecondary Institutions in Fall 2000: Statistical Analysis Report* (NCES 2004–010). Washington, D.C.: U.S. Department of Education, 2003.

DOLORES PERIN *is associate professor of psychology and education at Teacher's College, Columbia University, and senior researcher at the Community College Research Center.*

4

*Community college faculty who teach developmental
English classes face numerous pedagogical challenges.
Graduate programs, in-service training, and professional
association activities help prepare faculty for these
challenges, but additional support is needed.*

Preparing Faculty to Meet the Needs of Developmental Students

Carol A. Kozeracki

Students who enroll in higher education with academic skills that are substantially below college level face an uphill battle to progress to college-level classes, much less to obtain a degree. According to Smittle (2003), "These students present enormous challenges to developmental educators that often far exceed those presented by traditional college students" (p. 10). Although community colleges have been the primary organizations to deliver higher education to underprepared students, Casazza reminds us, "Access without the appropriate support is a false opportunity" (1999, p. 6). Central to developmental students' academic success is the presence of a well-trained, dedicated, and respected faculty.

Community college developmental instructors' abilities to respond to the needs of their students depends on the knowledge, training, and experience they bring to the classroom. This chapter, based on interviews with thirty-six developmental English instructors, presents the challenges faculty experience in their classes; describes their perceptions of the effectiveness of graduate programs, college-based development activities, and professional associations in supporting their teaching efforts; and offers recommendations for improving the professional development process for developmental faculty in community colleges (Kozeracki, 2004). The seven community colleges in this study are located in two states (one on the East Coast and one on the West Coast), have large enrollments (in excess of fifteen thousand students), and have varied organizational structures for their developmental programs (centralized, decentralized, and mixed models, as discussed by Perin in Chapter Three).

NEW DIRECTIONS FOR COMMUNITY COLLEGES, no. 129, Spring 2005 © Wiley Periodicals, Inc.

39

Challenges of Teaching Developmental Courses

Given the large number of underprepared students enrolling in community colleges, it is not surprising that their backgrounds and reasons for needing precollege courses are extremely varied. Hardin (1988) identifies six categories of students who require developmental coursework: poor choosers, adult learners, ignored students, foreign students, handicapped students, and "users" who lack clear-cut goals and are attending college more for purposes of avoidance than achievement. Each type of student brings different needs to the classroom, which should be addressed by specific pedagogical skills and knowledge. In addition, Maxwell (as cited in Piper, 1998) points out that many students resent being placed in developmental courses, especially if they received good grades in high school classes.

The faculty described in this chapter cite a similar range of challenges that students bring to the classroom: a lack of preparation, maturity, and motivation to do college work; language difficulties that should be addressed in English as a Second Language (ESL) classes rather than developmental English classes; learning disabilities that may never have been diagnosed; socioeconomic conditions that make it very difficult for students to progress academically; and anger over being placed in developmental classes.

A large percentage of those who enroll in developmental classes are traditional-age students who recently graduated from high school. In describing these students, instructors tend to distinguish two groups: those who attended poor public high schools and were never taught the basics of grammar and writing, and those who were exposed to good instruction but did not pay attention. As one instructor notes, "Most of my students are fairly recent high school graduates, which shocks me, because if you could see their test scores, even if you just take that as one measure, and their problems with their life skills, it is unbelievable to me. To me, it's an extreme crisis that these students are at that level."

Non-native English speakers, including both international students and native and immigrant students whose first language is not English, make up a growing proportion of the developmental population in many community colleges. Faculty without a background in ESL may not feel competent to address the needs of these students but still bear the responsibility for instructing them. Most colleges offer ESL classes, but some do not mandate ESL placement if students prefer to enroll in English classes, and some students who have taken and passed ESL classes are still not ready, in the instructors' views, for English courses.

Just as faculty express concern over their lack of expertise in working with students whose first language is not English, they also are worried about the growing need to be able to diagnose and teach students with learning disabilities. Faculty indicate that students with diagnosed learning disabilities and those with symptoms consistent with a diagnosis appear regularly in their classes. "Generally [we] see more students with learning disabilities and differences in developmental than we do in Comp. 1," says one instructor. Another professor states, "I would say it's not unusual in a developmental class of nineteen students to have four or five [with learning disabilities]." Some faculty have taken courses to help them address the challenges of working with students with disabilities, and others have learned how to work with them through years of experience and guidance from staff in the offices of disabled students. Some new faculty, however, are very concerned that they do not know how to properly serve these students.

A number of faculty point out that there is a link between their students' achievement levels and the socioeconomic conditions in which they live:

> Here's one thing that stands out: the bleak economic realities of their lives deeply affect their ability to profit from their classes. Most of them are working full-time, forty and up hours a week. Others are working thirty hours a week. Most students work, especially at the [lowest] level. They work because it's an economic necessity. And, not all of them, but a high percentage of them, are dependent on public transportation, or they drive cars in such bad repair that they are constantly breaking down, and then they are back to public transportation. Also, if they've come out of the public school system here in this country they're used to having books provided for them. Suddenly, they have to lay out possibly over $50 for one class. And it's a big issue, getting everyone to get a book before it becomes too hopelessly late for them.

A number of community college developmental instructors mention that even the most motivated students can be derailed by the need to work long hours outside the classroom, especially those who must work full-time. Serious family and health problems also seem to be common among these students, and can interfere with their ability to attend class and study.

Instructors are clearly sympathetic to the struggles and obstacles that students face as a result of their lower socioeconomic status. Many express admiration for the students who persist despite these challenges, but they also indicate that these societal conditions have a negative impact on students' readiness to learn, and thus, add to the instructor's teaching responsibilities.

Finally, faculty interviewed for this study are in accord with literature that shows students often enter developmental classes with negative attitudes about schooling in general and about developmental courses in particular. Most community college faculty must work hard to motivate students to show up for class, complete homework assignments, participate in classes, and commit themselves to doing their work. In developmental classes, this motivational role is even more pronounced. In addition, the gap between high school graduation standards and college entry standards is sometimes substantial, and some students are understandably confused or resentful if they must go from an honors high school English class to a basic writing course in college. Figuring out how to move students beyond their anger can be difficult for faculty.

Not unexpectedly, some faculty talk about a wearying sense of frustration that results from what they perceive to be a lack of student effort or commitment to the learning process, a sense that they are willing to work harder on their students' behalf than the students are willing to work themselves.

As this section of the chapter indicates, students entering community college developmental classes bring with them a number of academic, social, and emotional challenges. The following sections explore the extent to which graduate programs, college development activities, and professional associations prepare faculty to address these needs.

The Knowledge Gap: What Is Not Taught in Graduate School

For many faculty, the knowledge they gained in their graduate programs is significantly different from the knowledge they need to teach developmental classes. In many cases, this gap arises because the instructors are not planning to teach developmental courses when they begin their graduate programs. They may enter a literature program because of a love of reading or writing, but it is unlikely they will be able to discuss Shakespeare or Melville with the students they serve on a daily basis. Even instructors who choose a more relevant path, such as a master's program in reading, encounter mismatches between what they learn and what they need in order to teach developmental courses because these programs tend to be oriented toward elementary and secondary school students. However, instructors who come from applied programs, including reading, ESL, education, writing, and linguistics, find that more of their graduate training assists them in their teaching.

In discussing graduate programs with community college developmental instructors, and especially when the conversation turns to hiring policies, a clear tension emerges between the widely respected literature degrees and the less prestigious but more pertinent education or reading degrees. One professor, who is taking classes toward a doctorate in education, expresses annoyance at her professors' refusal to focus on the applied value of her studies. "Somehow I got the impression, 'Don't worry about pedagogy. Don't worry about the classroom. Let's not focus on that. Let's just take it as it is.' To me, I can't work like that. For me everything emerges from the classroom. The research that I do, the projects that I do, everything comes from the classroom."

Several instructors admit that they like the practicality of their program, even though, as one says, "I'm afraid of the connotations of that word." Time and again, instructors point to practical concepts that they are glad they learned, or that they are sorry were not offered in graduate school. The three issues that were most commonly mentioned as being important to instructors were grammar, pedagogy, and the needs of disabled students.

Many faculty members are talented writers who may find it difficult to explain basic concepts to students when they begin teaching. One relatively new full-time professor with a literature degree explains, "Beyond saying, 'That's not how you write that,' I don't know how to teach that stuff. And I wish there had been a 'This Is How You Teach Grammar' class in my grad program, because we didn't do that at all." Another instructor, a part-timer from a nineteenth-century American literature program. is equally blunt in describing her lack of preparation. "If you have an interest in writing, which I always have, then just teaching people how to write from the experience of having read a lot myself [is possible]. But I don't have any training whatsoever in this area." The instructors who took classes that defined grammatical concepts and explained how to convey them to non-English majors feel that they are at a great advantage when teaching students in developmental courses.

Similarly, basic teaching strategies—including presentation skills, lesson planning, and assessment strategies—are frequently not covered in graduate school, causing faculty to feel they are "fumbling and bumbling" during their first semester in front of a class. One instructor states, "The stuff I needed to learn from scratch was how to structure the class, what to have students do at home, what to do in the classroom, presentation ideas, structuring the classroom." Faculty who were able to participate in a clinical experience or spent time student teaching feel they gained much needed experience, practical knowledge. and confidence from that part of their graduate training.

Finally, a large number of faculty express a desire for formal training on how to address the needs of students with disabilities. A number mention that this topic should be addressed at the graduate level, and one professor indicates that if she were starting out today, she would concentrate her graduate study in this area.

A handful of graduate programs in developmental education now exist, but many of the instructors interviewed would probably find the curriculum to be too narrowly tailored because almost all of them enjoy teaching classes at both the college and precollege level. Therefore, it seems likely that graduate schools will continue to serve as only the first step in the process of faculty preparation, and individual colleges and the professional associations will retain the largest responsibility for teaching faculty how to work with underprepared students.

Recommendations for Graduate Training

Faculty identify a number of areas where graduate training could more adequately prepare them for their teaching responsibilities. Although courses in pedagogy are integral to graduate programs in education, faculty who have served on hiring committees indicate there is still a general preference to hire individuals with English degrees rather than education degrees.

Therefore, universities should include one or more pedagogy courses in English programs that primarily produce college instructors. These courses should address both general teaching strategies and skills such as grammar that are specific to teaching English. In addition, graduate programs in special education should incorporate strategies for dealing with college-age students with disabilities, instead of focusing exclusively on elementary and secondary school students. College instructors must also become familiar with strategies that can facilitate the success of adult students with disabilities, some of whom are not diagnosed when they enroll in college and, consequently, are unaware of the reason they are struggling in classes or the support available to assist them.

Faculty Development at the Community College

In order to provide successful faculty development programs, colleges must have strong administrative support, including appropriate rewards for participation, but faculty must also take ownership of the programs (Murray, 2001). Angelo (1994) recommends an approach that focuses on improving student learning rather than teaching; promotes faculty and student self-awareness, self-assessment, and self-improvement; and helps faculty understand how traditional research might be applied to their particular courses and students. Maxwell and Kazlauskas (1992) cite a number of effective practices in faculty development: expert consultation with colleagues on specific teaching matters, growth contracts or professional development plans, small grants for developing new teaching methods, faculty exchange programs with other institutions, funds for travel and attending professional meetings, and temporary course load reductions.

Unfortunately, Murray's (2001) national study reveals that there is "no evidence that faculty development at most community colleges is anything more than a randomly grouped collection of activities lacking intentional coordination with the mission of the college or the needs of faculty members" (p. 497). Grubb and Associates (1999) similarly report that faculty are overloaded and isolated, partly in deference to the principle of academic freedom, partly due to the proliferation of part-time faculty and lecturers, and partly because of the lack of activities to draw instructors together around teaching.

At the seven colleges included in this study, faculty development takes place in three venues: formal collegewide programs, official department meetings and activities, and informal conversations among colleagues. The most frequently offered collegewide programs are flex days, which are usually offered at the beginning of each academic year or semester. Colleges generally invite one or more speakers to address the faculty as a group, schedule time for departmental meetings, and allow faculty to participate in elective sessions on topics ranging from the use of technology to personal financial planning. Although substantial financial and human resources are invested in developing and offering these programs, instructors generally view them indifferently or negatively.

The literature provides some insight as to why this is the case. First, as Murray (2001) contends, if faculty development is to be successful, professors must have primary responsibility for the programs. Many faculty feel that programs similar to the one described in the preceding paragraph are engineered by administrators who are not knowledgeable about their professional needs. Instructors particularly resent being herded into a room at the beginning of each academic year to listen to a pep talk given by an outside speaker.

In contrast to administrator-led professional development seminars, activities that take place at the departmental level have tremendous potential for improving faculty teaching because they provide opportunities for interaction and discussion, a manifestation of what Bennett calls "the lively community of scholars" (1998, p. 22). Faculty in this study note the importance of collegial interaction—both structured and spontaneous—in their own departments.

In reporting what happens at department meetings, one instructor says, "Of course, if you ask any teacher what do they want, they all want to talk about what works, and share ideas, and be creative. But we just don't seem to make the time, or have the time, to do that." In most cases, department meetings are "business-oriented" and do not allow for discussions of pedagogy. Therefore, faculty development discussions are more likely to take place at dedicated sessions, such as organized roundtables, or through meetings of instructors who teach the same course. These tend not to be scheduled regularly but are highly regarded when they do occur, especially by new faculty.

Similarly, unscheduled hallway and office conversations remain a central source of learning for faculty. Across the seven campuses, there is a clear consensus that the informal sharing of information among colleagues is a tremendous socializing experience. As one professor reports, "Most important is really informal contact with colleagues." Frequent, easy access to colleagues is necessary if these types of interactions are to occur. Unfortunately, opportunities for these types of conversations are substantially reduced for part-time faculty, especially those without offices, and for instructors whose offices or classrooms are not in close proximity to those of their colleagues.

Thus, although we know that faculty interaction and discussions lead to faculty growth and development, logistical challenges tend to impede these types of interactions. Time constraints and other departmental requirements minimize opportunities for formal meetings with colleagues, and thus little time is available for teaching-related discussions. In addition, faculty who could most benefit from informal interactions—namely, part-timers and those who are physically isolated from their colleagues—are often unintentionally excluded from the spontaneous sharing that takes place in offices and hallways.

Recommendations for Professional Development

Most colleges require their instructors to participate in flex day activities each academic year. However, faculty feel that two components of many of these programs—motivational sessions led by outside speakers and programs addressing such areas as personal finance or fitness—are not worthwhile. However, faculty do identify professional development activities that are useful and should be emphasized or expanded. First, more time should be made for departmental meetings in which faculty discuss pedagogical issues. Second, colleges should recruit outside speakers who address issues that are of genuine concern to the whole faculty. Such topics include policy, budgets, the needs of students with learning disabilities, and how to incorporate learning and other educational theories into classroom practice. Third, faculty call for more opportunities to interact with professors from other disciplines whom they might not otherwise encounter.

In addition to suggestions for flex days, faculty make four other recommendations for college-based professional development. First, colleges should consider setting aside an hour or two each week when no classes meet to encourage a greater number of instructors to attend departmental meetings. Second, workshops or roundtables developed by instructors and presented to their colleagues can be extremely useful. By encouraging these types of sessions to be scheduled once or twice a semester, colleges will not only foster professional development but may also boost faculty morale. Similarly, faculty should be encouraged and supported to participate in local conferences sponsored by university or college consortia. These low-cost sessions provide faculty with opportunities for networking and gaining fresh perspectives, and because they are designed to meet the needs of participating institutions, they may be more relevant than some of the sessions presented at national conferences.

As this chapter demonstrates, new and experienced instructors share much information during informal conversations. Giving part-timers space to hold office hours, check e-mail, and make phone calls not only supports their teaching responsibilities but also increases the likelihood of their having instructive, casual conversations with colleagues. One option for achieving this goal, as suggested by an instructor, is for full-time faculty to allow part-timers to use their offices when the full-timers do not need them. Finally, it would be useful for each college to survey its faculty to learn about their development needs, rather than relying on the administration or committees to create faculty development programs.

The Role of the Professional Organizations

Findings from this study (Kozeracki, 2004) indicate that the typical instructor belongs to one or two professional associations, sporadically reads the journals they publish, and if full-time, attends a conference or workshop every year or two. Faculty are more likely to be affiliated with associations in the disciplines of English or composition than in the field of developmental education, usually because they teach at both the developmental and the college level and identify themselves as English rather than developmental instructors. College support for conference attendance varies tremendously by institution; some faculty receive funding to attend several conferences per year, whereas others do not receive support for any conference that requires an airplane flight or a hotel stay.

Instructors insist in their interviews that "practical is more useful." Not surprisingly, most developmental faculty focus on the pedagogical strategies outlined in journals and conference presentations. Some faculty convey an interest in research, but they are usually looking for a bridge between theory and practice. Faculty are turned off by the structure and language used in much of the theoretical writing in the field of education. However, they are receptive to writings that translate new theoretical perspectives into ways to improve classroom practice. One instructor talks about the value of Angelo and Cross's (1993) work: "It's so applicable, it's really a joy to look at some of that stuff. There's this preeminent researcher who's actually doing something we can use. It takes nothing to put that into practice. Whereas when you read some of this other stuff—never in a million years will that be useful to you." Angelo (1994) has suggested that one of the goals of faculty development programs should be to help instructors understand how traditional research might be applied to their particular courses and students, but this recommendation has yet to be widely implemented.

Another limitation of professional development activities and publications sponsored by academic associations is that the ideas presented in the conferences and publications tend not to circulate beyond the individual who reads the journal or attends the sessions. Even though Grubb and Associates (1999) stress the "value of collective approaches" (p. 199) in improving developmental education at the community colleges, most community colleges do not have an effective system in place for instructors to pass along the useful information they may gain from a conference or journal. Part-time faculty in particular, who are not usually eligible for support to attend conferences themselves, are also not able to interact informally with other instructors who have been to conferences and might have useful information to share.

Recommendations for Professional Associations

Faculty offer many suggestions for improving the value of the professional development sessions provided by the disciplinary associations. First, they call for an integration of scholarship and teaching, which, as Boyer (1990) notes, can help translate theoretical knowledge into meaningful applications that benefit students. Similarly, Astin (1998) suggests: "Research on programs for underprepared students and preparation of faculty to teach such students should be a collaborative effort carried out at the systems level" (p. 13). A commitment to bridging research and practice provides a tremendous opportunity for instructors to pursue scholarship and teaching strategies that can positively affect students.

Second, community colleges should facilitate the sharing of information from journals and conferences. One approach would be to order departmental subscriptions to key journals. Another alternative would be to encourage faculty members to e-mail colleagues about relevant journal articles. Similarly, colleges might ask conference attendees to alert colleagues to useful papers or presentations or share information about outstanding projects at other colleges. In addition, if a particular concept or program from a conference or journal is relevant to a number of faculty, colleges might schedule an informal discussion, roundtable, or workshop on the topic in order to share best practices.

Finally, faculty are more likely to be affiliated with English and composition-based associations, such as the National Council of Teachers of English or the Two-Year College English Association, than with the major developmental education associations, specifically the National Association for Developmental Education (NADE) and the College Reading and Learning Association (CRLA). Given their limited funds for conference participation, faculty in this study choose to belong to the organizations that address their teaching needs for both their developmental and college-level courses. In order to reach these faculty with the latest research and findings on developmental education, NADE and CRLA members should present at the broader English conferences and look for opportunities to publish in their journals.

Conclusion

The insights provided by faculty in this study reinforce the assertion in the literature that teaching underprepared college students is a challenging enterprise. The instructors indicate that a substantial gap exists between what they learn in graduate school and what they need to know to facilitate student learning. They identify three areas that should receive greater emphasis in graduate programs: instruction in how to teach basic grammar, pedagogical information on lesson planning and presentation, and strategies for recognizing and working with students with learning disabilities.

College-sponsored faculty development takes place through formal collegewide programs, department meetings and roundtables, and informal discussions among colleagues. Faculty are most satisfied with departmental activities that respond to issues they face in the classroom, and with informal discussions among colleagues. In discussing the value of professional associations, faculty are most interested in discovering strategies that can be applied directly to their teaching and are least interested in purely theoretical articles and presentations that do not offer practical applications to the developmental classroom. A common theme expressed by faculty is the central importance of informal communication among colleagues; colleges should look for opportunities to facilitate such discussions.

References

Angelo, T. A. "From Faculty Development to Academic Development." *AAHE Bulletin*, 1994, 46(10), 3–7.

Angelo, T. A., and Cross. K. P. *Classroom Assessment Techniques: A Handbook for College Teachers.* San Francisco: Jossey-Bass, 1993.

Astin. A. "Remedial Education and Civic Responsibility." *National Crosstalk*, 1998, 6(3), 12–13.

Bennett, J. B. *Collegial Professionalism: The Academy, Individualism, and the Common Good.* Phoenix, Ariz.: Oryx Press, 1998.

Boyer, E. L. *Scholarship Reconsidered: Priorities of the Professoriate.* San Francisco: Jossey-Bass, 1990.

Casazza, M. E. "Who Are We and Where Did We Come From?" *Journal of Developmental Education*, 1999, 23(1), 2–7.

Grubb, W. N., and Associates. *Honored but Invisible: An Inside Look at Teaching in Community Colleges.* New York: Routledge, 1999.

Hardin, C. J. "Access to Higher Education: Who Belongs?" *Journal of Developmental Education*, 1988, 12(1), 2–6, 19.

Kozeracki, C. A. "The Socialization of Community College Instructors Who Teach Developmental English." UMI Dissertation Services, UMI no. 3135549, 2004.

Maxwell, W. E., and Kazlauskas, E. J. "Which Faculty Development Methods Really Work in Community Colleges? A Review of Research." *Community/Junior College Quarterly*, 1992, 16(4), 351–360.

Murray, J. P. "Faculty Development in Publicly Supported Two-Year Colleges." *Community College Journal of Research and Practice*, 2001, 25(7), 487–502.

Piper, J. "An Interview with Martha Maxwell." *Learning Assistance Review*, 1998, 3(1), 32–39.

Smittle, P. "Principles for Effective Teaching in Developmental Education." *Journal of Developmental Education*, 2003, 26(3), 10–16.

Carol A. Kozeracki is assistant director of the Institute for the Study of Educational Entrepreneurship at UCLA.

5

Developmental learning community programs that are respectful of students' circumstances, supportive of their educational aims, and thoughtful about the purpose of education can be extremely effective in helping developmental students achieve their educational goals.

Learning Communities and Curricular Reform: "Academic Apprenticeships" for Developmental Students

Gillies Malnarich

In the beginning, potential; in the end, results. With these few words, the president of Saint Augustine's College (North Carolina), one of the first Historically Black colleges in the country, describes what her college has stood for since its founding in 1867. The college's mission conveys an optimistic determination that rests on a simple observation everyone is an able learner, and our job as educators is to figure out how best to support and stimulate students' desire to learn.

Eighty years after Saint Augustine's welcomed its first students, the Truman Commission on Higher Education called for the establishment of locally controlled colleges so all citizens—regardless of race, gender, religion, geographical location, or financial condition—could benefit from at least two years of postsecondary education. This declaration eventually led to the great expansion of community colleges, or "democracy's colleges," many established through the organizing efforts of local citizens' groups. The founding principle of these institutions, access to everyone "who can profit from instruction" (Roueche and Roueche, 1993. p. 25), continues to attract educators passionate about democratizing higher education.

Just how effective have community colleges been at turning access into academic success? At first glance, our collective report card is uneven at best. A decade ago, over half of all students enrolled in higher education dropped out during their first year at college (Tinto, Goodsell-Love, and Russo, 1993). Today, the first-year attrition rate at two-year colleges hovers at 45 percent compared with 26 percent at four-year colleges (Lamkin,

2004). These figures, augmented by local campus attrition data, serve as a backdrop for introducing learning communities as an educational reform strategy known for its dramatic impact on student retention rates (Taylor and Associates, 2003).

The Washington Center for Improving the Quality of Undergraduate Education uses the term *learning communities* to encompass various approaches to curricular reform that depart from the usual pattern of instructors teaching separate classes in separate subjects to separate groups of students. Learning communities intentionally restructure students' time, credit, and learning experiences to build community among students and faculty and to build curricular connections across disciplines, professional and technical programs, and skill areas. In the context of developmental education, learning communities restructure curriculum where student need is greatest; that is, those courses or areas of the curriculum where students often flounder and fail. Learning communities create the kind of learning environments that engage students in the hard, persistent, and challenging work associated with academic success.

This chapter begins with an overview of what it means to be "at risk" in higher education, which is a starting point for examining learning community practice in relation to three complementary strands of research: key factors associated with educational completion, students' conceptions of their own abilities and the implications for persistence, and the effects of collaborative pedagogy on student engagement. This research informs the different learning community approaches, described later in this chapter, that have been designed to turn potential into results—in developmental education, between developmental education and college level studies, and across the community college curriculum.

Being "At Risk" in Higher Education: The Context for Learning Communities

The promise of equitable educational opportunity for all confronts an undeniable reality: many entering students will not be ready for college because of a variety of external barriers that reduce their chances for academic success even before they attend their first class.

A first barrier, continuing patterns of separation and discrimination, refers to systemic class exclusion and racial segregation: impoverished neighborhoods, poorly funded schools, and curriculum stripped of its academic content. As McCabe (2000) indicates, "Poverty has the highest correlation with educational underpreparedness at every level, from preschool to graduate school" (p. 12).

Another barrier to academic success is the one-size-fits-all approach to learning and assessment that contributes to the estrangement of students who are expected to adjust to an academic culture not designed with them in mind, at places where they do not feel at home. Very few higher education institutions know how to maximize the intellectual and leadership potential of all their students, or what Tatum (2004) refers to as the ABCs of creating effective learning environments: affirming identity, building community, and cultivating leadership.

A third barrier, the misalignment of high school work with college-level expectations, describes a common situation where even those students with good high school grades are not ready for college. Among high school students who intend to continue their education, only 67 percent earn standard high school diplomas and only 42 percent graduate with college entry skills (McCabe, 2000).

Educational opportunity is also tied to affordability. Two recent government reports, *Access Denied* and *Empty Promises: The Myth of College Access in America* (Advisory Committee on Student Financial Assistance, 2001, 2002), indicated that the opportunity gap between income groups is wider than it was thirty years ago. In the mid-1970s the total price of a four-year public college education as a share of family income was 42 percent; this proportion climbed to a staggering 70 percent by 2003. Underfunding of education, rising tuition costs, and reduced financial aid have prevented hundreds of thousands of high school graduates from enrolling in higher education (Fitzgerald, 2004).

In addition, many community college students now work more than thirty hours a week, attend school part-time, raise children as single parents, pay for college, care for children at home, and worry about the affordability of going to school, all of which makes them less likely to meet their educational goals (Community College Survey of Student Engagement, 2002). An added liability, being a first-generation student, is overshadowed by the most telling risk factor of all, academic preparation. The more students need developmental education, the less likely they will stay in school, persist, and graduate (Adelman, 1999; Astin, 1985; Maxwell, 1979).

Findings from a national survey conducted in fall 2001 indicate that the need for developmental education is great among community college students. For instance, eighteen states estimated that 40 percent or more of entering college students need developmental education, although this average masks a broad spectrum: in some colleges the estimate is as low as 10.4 percent; in others it is as high as 70.9 percent (Education Commission of the States, 2002).

Key Factors Associated with Educational Completion: Implications for Developmental Curricula

Adelman (1999) identifies three factors that contribute most to degree completion. First, "academic intensity and quality of secondary school curriculum" are more critical than either socioeconomic status or precollege academic indicators such as test scores, class rank, or academic GPA (p. 84). Second, students who successfully complete higher levels of mathematics have a greater likelihood of completing a degree Third, students who require developmental reading are less likely to complete their degrees than students who take other types of developmental classes. The critical importance of intensity and quality of high school curriculum in ensuring successful transition from secondary school to college-level work and eventual degree completion led Adelman (1999) to conclude that "opportunity to learn" inside and outside school makes all the difference in whether students will be successful in their studies.

For developmental educators, the message could not be more clear: curriculum quality is the bridge between students' often inadequate and poor educational experience in high school and difficult college-level courses. Educational programs for developmental students must be engaging, substantive, and purposeful; they should serve as an intense, abbreviated "academic apprenticeship" where the habits of mind and the cluster of abilities associated with academic success are learned (Malnarich and Associates, 2003).

Several studies on developmental education describe best practices for providing quality developmental curricula. Noteworthy are early studies by Cross (1971, 1976) that emphasize the use of college-level materials, even for struggling students. In *Beyond the Open Door* (1971), Cross is highly critical of academic programs that focus on student deficiencies instead of building on student potential. She argues that students who consistently place in the bottom third of their class based on traditional tests of academic achievement and traditional curricula, are not "less skillful" than others but approach learning differently and often avoid learning something new because they fear failure.

In a follow-up study, Cross (1976) examines thirty years of research on effective ways to work with underprepared students and concludes that "skills training must be integrated into the other college experiences of the student" (p. 42) because there is no evidence that learning generic skills has any transferability. She also recommends that students in developmental courses have the opportunity to earn college credit as an incentive for taking the risk to learn something new. Similarly, Roueche and Roueche (1999) note that exemplary programs for academically underprepared students marry access and academic excellence and that curricular coherence is a criterion for excellence.

One of the most effective intervention strategies in developmental education, supplemental instruction (Boylan, 2002), targets high-risk courses rather than at-risk students. This model is implemented in courses where 30 percent or more students receive a D or F as a final grade or withdraw from the course, and supplements each course with regularly scheduled, weekly study sessions. These sessions are held outside class time, are open to any interested student, and are led by peer facilitators who successfully completed the course in the previous term. The supplemental instruction sessions help incoming students in a timely, discipline-specific way that is free from the stigma of remediation. During study sessions, students work collaboratively on course-generated assignments and problems. By 1999, more than 250,000 students participated in supplemental instruction (Arendale, 2002).

Like supplemental instruction, learning communities for developmental students need to be intentionally located in curricular trouble spots. Such "at risk" locations in the academy include high-risk courses where 30 percent or more of students drift away after one month, graveyard courses where 50 percent or more of students earn low grades or drop out, gateway courses that have a reputation among students for being tough, platform courses for entry into professional and technical programs, and transition courses for developmental students and second language speakers who are moving into college-level courses. We need to be especially attentive to patterns among students considered at risk in higher education. In particular, we should examine whether students earn the credits they sign up for, whether required courses are repeated by a particular group of students, and whether racial and ethnic groups are underrepresented in some courses but overrepresented in others.

An understanding of these issues, along with data about high-risk courses and analyses of where students struggle most in a course and why, form the basis for deciding what kind of learning community intervention would lead to improved student learning. For instance, Spokane Falls Community College's (Washington) robust "Learning How to Learn" community began with a link between its developmental study skills program and a difficult transfer-level biology course. Lane Community College (Oregon) integrated two high-failure courses for majors in the health occupations—chemistry and cell biology—into "BioBonds: Building Blocks for Your Body," which became a prerequisite and a requirement for the associate degree in nursing. Fayetteville Technical Community College (North Carolina) created an integrated module for introductory algebra and basic chemistry to stem the high failure rate in these developmental courses. The college soon created more modules, and eventually, a team-taught course. In all of these learning communities, student retention and persistence increased dramatically (Fogarty, Dunlap, and Associates, 2003; Malnarich and Associates, 2003).

Students' Conceptions of Their Own Abilities and Persistence: Developing Potential Based on High Expectations

Recently, several scholars have examined students' academic motivation and self-theories about their abilities as learners. Dweck (2000) notes that self-theories, even more than self-confidence, influence students' approaches to learning. In formal educational contexts, for instance, students tend to adopt achievement goals that are either learning- or performance-oriented.

Learning-oriented goals focus on increasing competence and deepening understanding, whereas performance goals center on "winning positive judgments of your competence and avoiding negative ones" (p. 48). These different outcomes reflect students' conceptions about intelligence and their own abilities. Performance-oriented students tend to adopt an "entity theory," where ability and intelligence are static and being good or not good at something is immutable and fixed; these students expect quick results with little effort. By contrast, learning-oriented students tend to adopt an "incremental theory," in which intelligence and ability are changeable and contingent; these students appreciate that learning is hard work.

Educators are also either entity theorists or incremental theorists, and their views influence how they assess students' abilities. As Grubb and Associates (1999) point out, a conventional approach to instruction is often based on the view that intelligence is fixed and one-dimensional, "that students who score poorly on diagnostic tests are deficient, lacking the skills and knowledge that would enable them to score at the right level. The language of deficiency is quite common in conventional instruction, particularly in remedial and developmental education" (p. 31).

However, as Smilkstein (2003) demonstrates, learning is not about deficits, but is, instead, about potential. In We're Born to Learn (2003), she summarizes findings from an extended participatory research project and highlights six main stages associated with the "brain's natural learning process" (p. 49). In all cases, practice (and more practice) over time is key to moving from not knowing how to do something, to becoming reasonably competent, to eventually achieving mastery. This analysis validates the incremental theory on the development of ability; learning is not held back until each step is mastered but is both developmental and reiterative. For instance, when we are learning to ride a two-wheel bicycle, we do not repeatedly practice the correct way to place our hands on the handlebars; we move onto the "real thing"—the chance to pedal a few yards on our own. Because learning communities purposefully restructure student and faculty time so the curriculum is less fragmented and more integrated, students have the opportunity to develop their abilities in an incremental way.

Effects of Collaborative Pedagogy on Student Engagement: The Case for Learning Communities

Learning communities have been credited with improving student engagement, persistence, and academic achievement (Astin, 1993; McCabe and Day, 1998; Tinto, Goodsell-Love, and Russo, 1993; Tinto, 1997). They are more than an instructional strategy; they represent an intentional departure from many traditional practices in higher education—including in developmental education—and their growth from marginal, isolated experiments to a national reform effort is well documented (Levine Laufgraben and Shapiro, 2004; Smith, MacGregor, Matthews, and Gabelnick, 2004).

Like other learning communities, those designed for developmental students vary based on the degree of curricular integration and degree of collaboration among faculty and staff. Three general patterns or structural frameworks for learning communities exist, including unmodified courses, linked or clustered courses, and team-taught learning communities. The common aim in all these frameworks is to foster explicit social and intellectual connections among people and ideas.

Unmodified Courses. In this type of learning community, ten to thirty students enroll in two or three larger and unmodified classes. They also enroll in an additional course that is available only to them. One adaptation of this model, freshman interest groups (FIGs), regroups students based on shared academic interests such as an interdisciplinary theme, a topic-based inquiry, or a major. The additional course might orient students to campus support services, allow for career exploration tied to academic advising, or offer course-related study groups, skill-based workshops, service learning projects, or field trips. FIGs may be led by teaching assistants, student peer mentors, academic advisers, counselors, faculty, or a teaching team, and credit hours can range from zero to three (Smith, MacGregor, Matthews, and Gabelnick, 2004).

Another adaptation, the integrative seminar or colloquy, uses the additional course to deepen student learning and build community through theme-based readings, discussions, and research projects. A faculty team—usually instructors of the larger classes—convenes the seminar. For instance, at one institution where 75 percent of beginning students need developmental courses, an "open to all" critical inquiry seminar introduces students to the expectations and requirements for successful college learning and provides transitional support for all students without stigmatizing those who are working on basic academic skills.

Linked or Clustered Classes. In this second type of learning community, students register together in two or more courses that are explicitly linked by content or theme. Faculty coordinate syllabi and assignments and intentionally foster community through social and curricular connections between the linked but distinct courses. Linked or paired courses are often scheduled back-to-back to facilitate collaborative work, and the time at the end of one class and the beginning of another provides an opportunity for the teaching team to collaboratively facilitate project work, seminars, and group presentations.

Often, introductory skill-building classes such as composition, speech, information literacy, and computer applications are linked to challenging content courses. When two or more courses are linked they are often referred to as a *cluster*. Both links and clusters enroll a "pure cohort," where the same twenty-five to thirty students attend both classes. Some links and clusters connect larger general education courses with smaller classes such as writing, study strategies, or speech, and the smaller classes incorporate the content of the larger class into their curricula. At La Guardia Community

College (New York), the New Student House program for ESL and developmental students includes two developmental courses (reading and writing), a college-level content course, and a freshman seminar taught by a counselor who meets weekly with the faculty team to evaluate student progress. In the semester prior to teaching in this program, the faculty team members plan the integrated curriculum and develop a joint syllabus that includes common readings, films, and field trips. They also design joint assignments using common materials, which allows each discipline to become a resource for the other (Malnarich and Associates, 2003).

Team-Taught Learning Communities. In team-taught learning communities, students enroll in a fully team-planned and team-taught program of study across disciplines and skill areas that usually focuses on an integrative theme, question, issue, or topic. Teaching teams sometimes include counselors, student affairs professionals, and librarians, and the teaching team's preparation for class constitutes its own learning community. Learning opportunities for students include seminars, internships, laboratory studies, service learning, and extended research projects. For instance, Skagit Valley College (Washington State) integrates Spanish and English grammar in "En Otros Terminos/In Other Words" (Fogarty, Dunlap, and Associates, 2003). De Anza Community College (California) integrates developmental reading, developmental writing, and an introduction to the visual arts in "Comics Speak Our Lives: The Graphic Novel Meets English 1A" (Malnarich and Associates, 2003).

Tinto, Goodsell-Love, and Russo (1993) published the first in-depth assessment of students' academic and social experience in learning communities as part of a national research project on student learning in higher education. They investigated the freshman interest group at the University of Washington, the coordinated studies program at Seattle Central Community College, and learning community clusters at La Guardia Community College. The results of this study drew educators' attention to the merits of collaborative pedagogy. First, when students are part of a cohort or community of peers, their attendance and participation improve, and the groups formed in class often meet outside class to study and socialize. Second, when students are exposed to intellectual and cultural diversity through team teaching and classroom activities, they feel encouraged to explore their own identity and find their own voice. Third, when students learn in collaborative settings, their academic performance and persistence increase. Finally, even when students attend large impersonal institutions or commute to school, collaborative learning is possible and works (Tinto, Goodsell-Love, and Russo, 1993). This fourth finding surprises many educators who do not associate learning communities with large inner-city community colleges.

In a comprehensive review of 150 research studies and assessment reports, Taylor and Associates (2003) reach similar conclusions: "Learning communities, structured in a variety of ways, are a proven and effective strategy for improving undergraduate education with respect to student persistence, performance, and perceptions of satisfaction and learning" (p. 66).

Recommendations for Creating Effective Learning Communities

In creating learning communities, the question "What do we want students to know and be able to do 'out there' that we are responsible for 'in here?'" can be considered in a longer time frame than a quarter or semester and in a broader context than that offered in traditional, fragmented developmental curricula (Malnarich and Lardner, 2003). Developmental learning community programs that are respectful of students' circumstances, supportive of their educational aims, and thoughtful about the purpose of education usually share a set of defining characteristics.

Infuse Intellectually Rigorous, Inclusive Curriculum with High Expectations. Programs that integrate skills with content, emphasize reading- and writing-intensive assignments, and use college-level materials help students learn how to do college-level work by actually having them do it. By combining intellectual rigor with skillful developmental pedagogy, faculty members indicate that they expect that students will be successful. At Grossmont Community College (California), students read, discuss, and write about a selection of engaging books that are respectful and representative of diverse cultural knowledge. The program's success is demonstrated by the growth of linked classes at the college, which totaled fifty in 2003. At Shoreline Community College (Washington State), students enrolled in "College Knowledge" develop a critical appreciation of academic culture through an in-depth study of classic readings from the humanities, arts, social sciences, and natural sciences (Malnarich and Associates, 2003).

Design Developmentally Appropriate Assignments and Award Fluid Credits. The shift from a curriculum based on decontextualized skills to one that emphasizes contextualized abilities allows students to work on developing essential knowledge as they engage in intellectually stimulating and often thematically based learning community work. At Seattle Central Community College, learning communities draw on the content of two or more introductory college-level courses and often include a component that awards ESL, developmental writing, or English composition credit based on the quality of students' written work. At De Anza Community College, students enroll in a large college-level lecture as well as one of three smaller writing cohorts (ESL, developmental English, or college English). The issues and questions emphasized in assignments are the same, but the expectations for paper length, references cited, and written expression are specific to each class.

Invite Student Participation in the Creation of Knowledge. By extending the definition of a learning community to include places where new knowledge is constructed, seminars and class discussions can offer unique opportunities for diverse students to learn across their own significant differences. For instance, faculty in La Guardia Community College's New Student House design classroom activities and make curricular choices that intentionally introduce non-Western experiences, language, and values into the classroom in order to disturb what people "know" to be true. Their students, already among the most diverse in the country, are invited to explore diversity and engage in comparative cultural analysis that upsets essentialist and monocultural notions of "truth" (Koolsbergen, 2001; van Slyck, 1997).

Fulfilling Student Potential

"One of the tasks of the progressive educator," Freire (1992) writes, "is to unveil opportunities for hope, no matter what the obstacles may be" (p. 9). A conversation with a team of developmental educators from Miami Dade College (Florida), at a workshop on designing learning communities, illustrates how developmental educators can help students realize "opportunities for hope." The faculty team described an integrated assignment they had designed to connect developmental reading, writing, and mathematics.

No longer skill-based and school-bound, the team freely explored new learning possibilities: What might the interdisciplinary theme or topic-based inquiry be? Who were their students? Where did they live? What issues did their communities face? By bringing their students' worlds into the classroom, the possibilities for their proposed learning community burst through the constraints of the academy. Students would become knowledgeable about a critical issue and become active in their communities; they would write informational pamphlets, conduct teach-ins, work with elementary and middle-school teachers; they would read, write, and decipher statistics in the interests of the people, for the people. Welcome to democracy's colleges and the yet unfulfilled dream. *In the beginning, potential; in the end, results.*

References

Adelman, C. *Answers in the Tool Box: Academic Intensity, Attendance Patterns, and Bachelor's Degree Attainment.* Washington, D.C.: U.S. Department of Education, Office of Educational Research and Improvement, 1999.

Advisory Committee on Student Financial Assistance. *Access Denied: Restoring the Nation's Commitment to Equal Educational Opportunity.* Washington, D.C.: Advisory Committee on Student Financial Assistance, 2001.

Advisory Committee on Student Financial Assistance. *Empty Promises: The Myth of College Access in America.* Washington, D.C.: Advisory Committee on Student Financial Assistance, 2002.

Arendale, D. "History of Supplemental Instruction (SI): Mainstreaming of Developmental Education." In D. B. Lundell and J. Higbee (eds.), *Histories of Developmental Education.* Minneapolis: Center for Research on Developmental Education and Urban Literacy, General College, University of Minnesota, 2002.

Astin, A. W. *Achieving Education Excellence: A Critical Assessment of Priorities and Practices in Higher Education.* San Francisco: Jossey-Bass, 1985.

Astin, A. *What Matters in College: Four Critical Years Revisited.* San Francisco: Jossey-Bass, 1993.

Boylan, H. R. *What Works: Research-Based Best Practices in Developmental Education.* Boone, N.C.: Continuous Quality Improvement Network with the National Center for Developmental Education, 2002.

Community College Survey of Student Engagement. *Engaging Community Colleges: A First Look.* Austin, Tex.: Community College Survey of Student Engagement, 2002. http://www.ccsse.org/publications/report.pdf. Accessed Nov. 16, 2004.

Cross, K. P. *Beyond the Open Door: New Students to Higher Education.* San Francisco: Jossey-Bass, 1971.

Cross, K. P. *Accent on Learning: Improving Instruction and Reshaping the Curriculum.* San Francisco: Jossey-Bass, 1976.

Dweck, C. S. *Self-Theories: Their Role in Motivation, Personality, and Development.* Philadelphia: Psychology Press, 2000.

Education Commission of the States, Center for Community College Policy. *State Policies on Community College Remediation: Findings from a National Survey.* Denver: Education Commission of the States, Center for Community College Policy, 2002.

Fitzgerald, B. K. "Missed Opportunities: Has College Opportunity Fallen Victim to Policy Drift?" *Change,* 2004, 36(4), 10–19.

Fogarty, J., Dunlap, L., and Associates. *Learning Communities in Community Colleges.* National Learning Communities Project Monograph Series. Olympia: The Evergreen State College, Washington Center for Improving the Quality of Undergraduate Education, in cooperation with the American Association of Community Colleges, 2003.

Freire, P. *Pedagogy of Hope: Reliving Pedagogy of the Oppressed.* New York: Continuum, 1992.

Grubb, W. N., and Associates. *Honored but Invisible: An Inside Look at Teaching in Community Colleges.* New York: Routledge, 1999.

Koolsbergen, W. "Approaching Diversity: Some Classroom Strategies for Learning Communities" *Peer Review,* 2001, Summer/Fall, 25–31.

Lamkin, M. D. "More Money Is Not Enough: Philanthropy Can Play a Unique Role in Providing Greater Access and Affordability in Higher Education." *Notebook,* Winter 2004, 2.

Levine Laufgraben, J., and Shapiro, N. *Sustaining and Improving Learning Communities.* San Francisco: Jossey-Bass, 2004.

Malnarich, G., and Associates. *The Pedagogy of Possibilities: Developmental Education, College-Level Studies, and Learning Communities.* National Learning Communities Project Monograph Series. Olympia: The Evergreen State College, Washington Center for Improving the Quality of Undergraduate Education, in cooperation with the American Association of Community Colleges, 2003

Malnarich, G., and Lardner, D. E. "Designing Integrated Learning for Students: A Heuristic for Teaching, Assessment, and Curriculum Design." *Washington Center for Improving the Quality of Undergraduate Education Occasional Paper,* 2003, Winter, 1.

Maxwell, M. *Improving Student Learning Skills: A Comprehensive Guide to Successful Practices and Programs for Increasing the Performance of Underprepared Students.* San Francisco: Jossey-Bass, 1979.

McCabe, R. H. *No One to Waste: A Report to Public Decision Makers and Community College Leaders.* Washington, D.C.: Community College Press, 2000.

McCabe, R. H., and Day, P. R. Jr. (eds.). *Developmental Education: A Twenty-First Century Social and Economic Imperative.* Mission Viejo. Calif.: League for Innovation in the Community College and the College Board, 1998.

Roueche, J. E., and Roueche, S. D. *Between a Rock and a Hard Place: The At-Risk Student in the Open Door College.* Washington, D.C.: Community College Press, 1993.

Roueche, J. E., and Roueche, S. D. *High Stakes, High Performance: Making Remedial Education Work.* Washington, D.C.: Community College Press, 1999.

Smilkstein, R. *We're Born to Learn: Using the Brain's Natural Learning Process to Create Today's Curriculum*. Thousand Oaks, Calif.: Corwin Press, 2003.

Smith, B. L., MacGregor, J., Matthews, R. S., and Gabelnick, F. *Learning Communities: Reforming Undergraduate Education*. San Francisco: Jossey-Bass, 2004.

Tatum, B. D. "Building a Road to a Diverse Society." *Chronicle of Higher Education,* 2004, *50*(30), B6.

Taylor, K., and Associates. *Learning Communities Research and Assessment: What We Know Now*. National Learning Communities Project Monograph Series. Olympia: The Evergreen State College, Washington Center for Improving the Quality of Undergraduate Education, in cooperation with the American Association of Community Colleges, 2003.

Tinto, V. "Classrooms as Communities: Exploring the Educational Character of Student Persistence." *Journal of Higher Education,* 1997, *68*(6), 599–623.

Tinto, V., Goodsell-Love, A., and Russo, P. "Building Community." *Journal of Liberal Education,* 1993, Fall, 16–21.

van Slyck, P. "Repositioning Ourselves in the Contact Zone." *College English,* 1997, *59*(2), 149–170.

GILLIES MALNARICH is codirector of the Washington Center for Improving the Quality of Undergraduate Education at The Evergreen State College.

This case study describes steps for implementing innovative learning communities that build basic skills and foster self-confidence in students at the developmental level.

6

Developmental Learning Communities at Metropolitan Community College

Susan Raftery

As increasing numbers of students with basic skills deficiencies enter community colleges, educators are often perplexed about how to address the needs of those who are unable to succeed in traditional classrooms. Given the likelihood that the developmental student has already had an unsatisfying twelve-year educational track record, it comes as little surprise that conventional methods are usually ineffective. Learning communities, which link or cluster classes around interdisciplinary themes and enroll common cohorts of students, provide community colleges with an enormous opportunity to change years of negative educational experiences into positive outcomes.

Metropolitan Community College (MCC) in eastern Nebraska has an open admissions policy with no mandatory assessment or placement requirements. However, students are strongly encouraged to take advantage of COMPASS and ASSET placement testing to ensure proper course assignment. Currently, MCC serves over twenty-five thousand students each year; roughly 50 percent of those who take the reading and English placement exams need basic skills development. Approximately six years ago, MCC decided to transform its developmental education offerings, and ultimately, the experiences of students who participate in the program. MCC's interest in finding ways to address students' actual learning challenges and their nonacademic barriers to learning led to the development of the Academic Improvement for Success program (AIM), a learning community initiative that has significantly improved success and retention rates for students with developmental needs. Although MCC offers a wide range of developmental courses in reading, math, English, and English as a Second Language (ESL), the AIM program provides assistance to students with multiple academic deficiencies by offering a level of support beyond what a student taking a stand-alone developmental course receives.

Development of AIM

Tinto's (1997) assertion that learning communities can have a positive influence on commuter students, and that students learn best when courses are integrated into a community of learners, set the stage for the development of MCC's early AIM program. MCC's first Developmental Education Task Force decided to integrate Tinto's work into their efforts to enhance the low success and retention rates of students with severe academic deficiencies. A commitment to understanding and employing educational theory played a significant role not only in shaping the initial program but also in modifying and enhancing AIM components over the years.

In both its developmental learning communities initiative and its general developmental education program, MCC takes a decentralized approach where faculty are not designated as developmental-level professors but rather as math, English, and reading faculty who teach both developmental and higher-level courses. One of AIM's early challenges was to ensure that instructors had an awareness of the needs of developmental students. Thus, MCC created strong faculty and staff development initiatives that remain central to the program. Task force members also recognized the need for support from top-level administrators in both educational and student services. Today a dean-level administrator is responsible for coordinating the program, and is assisted by two other deans' offices.

A third essential component of the original program was the integration of student services personnel. Although many learning community models do not incorporate these practitioners, AIM includes a retention counselor on each campus team to address the nonacademic barriers that many MCC students face. The counseling component has proven vital to student success, because financial, social, and emotional barriers frequently must be addressed before students can overcome academic barriers. At MCC, counselors meet with students individually, make class presentations about college procedures such as course enrollment processes, and often teach a learning strategies course or module as part of the program.

Nearly 80 percent of individuals taking the math placement exam at MCC need at least one developmental course. Because MCC does not have mandatory placement, counselors and advisers must give students an effective rationale for enrolling in the courses they need. It appears that these advising strategies have paid off; 8,336 MCC students took developmental courses during the 2002–03 academic year.

Over the years, MCC has refined its developmental processes and modified the original AIM model by learning from what has worked and what has not. Early on, the college recognized the need to recruit highly qualified faculty and staff to the program, and this practice has remained. AIM recruits individual professors to participate, rather than simply sending a blanket appeal to instructors. AIM faculty qualifications include excellent peer and student evaluations, good rapport with students, and an overall willingness to be flexible and to share everything, from class time to teaching materials. Although instructors maintain autonomy in their classrooms, they are expected to communicate with their team members and come to consensus on classroom management issues and program expectations.

AIM Components

The AIM learning community is designed to help students improve basic skills, develop sound learning strategies, and set realistic goals before beginning college-level coursework. AIM uses the supportive environment of a learning community to build skills and foster self-confidence in those students who are most at risk. Faculty, counselor, and classmate support makes AIM ideal for students who are unsure of their abilities, and it allows them to receive the instruction and encouragement they need to succeed.

AIM offers students many advantages: a block schedule that allows students to enroll as a cohort in two or more reading, math, writing, and personal or career development courses during a one-quarter program; a campus-based team of professionals who provide a strong system of academic and counseling support; diagnostic testing; interdisciplinary approaches to instruction; career exploration; cultural and extracurricular activities; and access to academic support services. Faculty and counselor teams meet regularly to discuss lesson plans and individual student progress. This regular interaction allows for immediate counselor intervention when problems arise, provides faculty with time to design integrated activities, and promotes a feeling of pride among team members when students overcome barriers and succeed.

Faculty members are each paid a $400 stipend during the first quarter that a new learning community is offered. The funding is not meant to pay for any specific activity but rather to acknowledge the extra time and effort required to develop a new interdisciplinary learning experience for students. Although some faculty teams offer highly integrated activities throughout the learning community experience, others choose to teach their courses more independently and tie the curriculum together through a few key activities that emphasize learning and employability skills, such as problem solving, teamwork, communication, and decision making.

Courses in the AIM program are the same as MCC's regular developmental offerings. By using the college's standard developmental courses, MCC avoids problems with financial aid and course quality. Students pay the same tuition for AIM courses as they would for any other developmental courses; however, they must enroll through a counselor intake process. This process ensures that students are placed into the proper developmental levels, have access to the support structures necessary to meet the demands of the program, and understand their role in the learning community experience (Boylan, 2002). With these goals in mind, the intake and enrollment processes include counselor assistance with filling out financial aid forms, conversations with students to address nonacademic barriers, and activities that help students acclimate to program expectations before classes begin.

Although AIM's budget—which is made up of small grants and allocations from the college's foundation—is minimal, it allows students to participate in extracurricular activities such as cultural events and field trips.

AIM Program Design

In the early years, AIM followed a fairly rigid block schedule that required students to sign up for four beginning-level developmental classes—reading, math, English, and learning strategies—for a total of fourteen credit hours over an eleven-week quarter. Recent modifications incorporated some of the best components of the program into more flexible options that enable a greater number of students to benefit from AIM's approach. The impetus for program modification came when MCC moved from offering only two developmental math courses to five. As it became more difficult to find enough students from each math course to meet enrollment targets for the block schedule, MCC created paired developmental reading and English classes, in which students from any of the five math courses could enroll.

Today the AIM program includes both the original four-course schedule and an option to participate in paired developmental reading and English classes or paired ESL courses. These pairings only require students to sign up for a minimum of seven credit hours, which allows those who attend part-time to participate in a learning community experience. If students wish to enroll in a developmental math or learning strategies course in addition to the paired courses, they may do so. However, these courses are not part of the closed paired-class cohort and are available to all students needing remedial assistance. A sample block schedule for the full fourteen-hour AIM program is shown in Figure 6.1.

AIM Innovations

The AIM program's early successes, coupled with the college's strong commitment to providing accessible developmental education at all three of its campuses, led MCC to apply to the U.S. Department of Education for a five-year Title III grant to strengthen its developmental education program. MCC is currently in the final year of the grant.

Title III funding has allowed for the modification and expansion of AIM components to enhance the entire developmental program and alter collegewide attitudes about learner-centered education. The grant has also made it possible for faculty to modify the developmental curriculum to

Figure 6.1. AIM for Success Schedule

Monday	Tuesday	Wednesday	Thursday
9:00–11:00 A.M. English	9:00–10:40 A.M. Reading	9:00–11:00 A.M. English	9:00–10:40 A.M. Reading
Open Study/ Tutoring	10:50–11:40 A.M. Success Strategies	Open Study/ Tutoring	10:50–11:40 A.M. Success Strategies
11:50–1:00 P.M. Math	11:50–1:00 P.M. Math	11:50–1:00 P.M. Math	11:50–1:00 P.M. Math

incorporate more active learning strategies. Facilities have been expanded to include math and writing centers in addition to existing learning centers. Most importantly, learning communities were recently added as a strategic initiative in the college's 2003–2006 strategic plan. As a result MCC has increased the number of learning communities available to students both at the developmental level and in various programs, recognizing that many students continue to struggle with basic skill competencies even after they complete developmental courses. The successful components of the AIM program have been key in shaping all of these initiatives.

Other recent innovations include retraining existing career counselors to provide academic assistance to students at the developmental level. Over the past two years, MCC has focused on teaming these academic counselors with all of the developmental reading instructors to assist them in teaching life skills and college orientation strategies to the students in their classes.

In the past, these academic counselors focused mainly on registering students on a first-come, first-served basis. Today, however, they offer long-term caseload assistance for the college's underprepared students. This move has led to a more integrated system in which faculty and staff work closely together on student development issues. Individualized student learning plans and an e-mail communication and referral system have been established to facilitate faculty and counselor communication about student concerns and to provide a way to refer students to college support services when needed.

AIM Outcomes

Students in AIM have flourished in the years since the program began: class attendance has improved, and course completion and retention rates have increased. In addition, because AIM helps students connect with the institution, students are more likely to seek help when they need it and to enroll in subsequent courses.

Course Success Rates. Using 2002–03 enrollment data, a study was conducted to compare the success rates of students taking developmental courses in the AIM program with those taking the same courses outside the learning community. The study involved 87 AIM students, 1,210 developmental English students, 1,053 developmental math students, and 632 developmental reading students.

Results revealed that 10 percent more of AIM students successfully completed developmental English and reading courses. However, 7 percent fewer AIM students were able to successfully complete the developmental math course than non-AIM students (see Table 6.1). Although results are not statistically significant, these findings are informative because the AIM students in the study were required to take all three developmental courses at once rather than one at a time as many developmental students do. This means that the AIM students, facing severe academic challenges in all three basic skills areas, performed as well as students needing developmental assistance in only one skill area, usually math. Although the study involved acceptable levels of student sampling, MCC must next measure the consistency of these outcomes over time and the influence of such factors as student age and the quarter in which the courses are taken.

Retention Rates. AIM retention and persistence rates are also impressive. AIM students persist for an average of five quarters, with a 90 percent retention rate after one quarter and a 74 percent retention rate after an academic year. Students in regular developmental English have an 81 percent retention rate for one quarter, and a 65 percent retention rate for the academic year. Similarly, students in regular developmental math average a 64 percent annual retention rate.

Grade Point Averages. Even more impressive, the average GPA for students moving from AIM courses into college-level courses is 2.3. The average GPA for all MCC students (both those in developmental and those in college-level courses) is 2.6. Thus, AIM students earn roughly the same grades, even though they tend to start out with academic deficiencies in all three basic skills areas.

The positive impact of linking student and educational services was highlighted in a recent study (Metropolitan Community College, 2003) that tracked developmental reading students who were assisted by an academic counselor. The study found an 11 percent increase in course success rates over two academic years. In addition, after just one year of including academic counselors in developmental reading courses, the number of students who went on to complete one or more college-level courses with a grade of C or better increased. The study also indicated increased success rates for those students who went on to take computer and health courses. MCC's initial goal was to have at least a 50 percent pass rate for its developmental reading students who attempted a college-level computer or health class. This goal was surpassed, as 71 percent of reading students who attempted one or more computer courses and 57 percent of reading students who attempted one or more health-related courses passed with a C or better (Metropolitan Community College, 2003).

Table 6.1. AIM Student Success Rates

	English		Reading		Math	
	AIM	Non-AIM	AIM	Non-AIM	AIM	Non-AIM
Student fails or withdraws at instructor's initiation.	10	14	9	9	11	10
Student passes.	71	61	75	65	58	65
Student reenrolls in same course	8	13	6	17	20	15
Student withdraws.	11	12	10	9	11	10

Note: Numbers are percentages.

Graduation Rates. AIM students have also demonstrated long-term success. Fifty-eight percent complete a minimum of thirty credit hours, and 29 percent complete at least seventy credit hours. This is especially notable because when these students enter MCC, their academic skills are among the lowest. A significant number of AIM students (about 8 percent) have gone on to earn associate degrees; the collegewide graduation rate for associate degrees is 8.9 percent. Although these statistics may seem low for both groups, it is important to note that MCC students enroll for a variety of reasons, including to update their skills, to pursue a one-year certificate, or to take courses that transfer to a four-year institution.

Student Satisfaction. Student satisfaction rates are also positive. Over 95 percent of AIM students indicate that they benefited from the program, and 98 percent say they would recommend AIM to a friend or family member. Because AIM students have a working relationship with all members of the campus team (instructors, counselors, and tutors), they feel a real connection to the college. They understand what support services are available and know where and how to access them. Because AIM is geared toward students who are new to the college, this program sets a positive tone for the rest of these students' academic experiences.

AIM's success and emerging reputation has led to program growth and expansion; enrollment has increased from 13 students in one learning community in fall 1998 to 107 students in seven developmental learning communities in fall 2004. Plans are also under way to offer at least four more AIM developmental learning communities by expanding to sites outside the college's three main campuses and offering evening options.

Lessons Learned

As AIM has evolved, MCC has learned many important lessons. First, the college learned that appropriate criteria should be established for student participation to increase students' likelihood of successfully completing the program. Students selected for developmental learning communities should test into the developmental level but above the Adult Basic Education level in all three basic skills areas, and they should also be able to make the financial, motivational, and time commitments necessary to attend multiple classes, complete homework, and balance other areas of responsibility successfully.

Second, MCC learned that faculty and staff must make the commitment to work in a team environment. The most effective teams have been willing to discuss and reach consensus on such issues as maintaining consistent attendance policies and holding team meetings with students who are in danger of failing. Teams have been most effective in meeting students' needs when a spirit of camaraderie and compromise exists. Students, faculty, and staff must all agree to support each other in these learning environments.

Establishing clear leadership has also been important. Campus teams are usually led by the counselor, who does the initial student intake, assists students with financial aid issues, plans a structured orientation session for students, and oversees team communication. A college administrator should be tasked with overall program development and coordination.

Despite AIM's success, MCC has learned that there will always be ongoing challenges, including finding ways to meet individual students' needs when so many financial, social, and emotional issues affect their academic progress. Although attrition rates among AIM students are lower than for those students in regular developmental courses, several AIM students drop out each quarter. Fortunately, many return later when they are able to devote the time necessary to succeed.

Finally, MCC was challenged by the heavy time commitment imposed by the original fourteen-credit-hour program; this issue, however, was addressed effectively by offering paired courses. These classes offer the same integrated approach to the curriculum and supportive team-learning environment, but they allow students who cannot or should not take a full course load to participate.

Best Practices

AIM has become a model for all of MCC's developmental course offerings, and many of the program's components have been incorporated into other courses so a greater number of students can benefit from a learning community approach. Over the years, MCC has developed a list of best practices that might assist other institutions wishing to initiate similar programs. They are as follows:

- Gain support from the administration.
- Recruit and invite highly qualified faculty and staff to participate.
- Integrate counselor support into every campus team, and encourage students to get to know counselors on a personal level.
- Schedule back-to-back classes (in clustered programs and throughout all developmental offerings).

- Include a tutoring component.
- Provide learning strategies classes or seminars.
- Develop an intake process by which counselors can provide an overview of program components, help students fill out financial aid forms, and address barriers such as transportation and child care.
- Restrict enrollment to students who need remedial assistance but score above Adult Basic Education levels.
- Make student services staff aware of learning community options and help them understand the value of these options so they can market programs to students.
- Provide a structured orientation on the first day of classes that outlines student and faculty expectations and classroom and attendance policies.
- Provide faculty and staff development opportunities to enhance understanding of the needs of underprepared students.
- Integrate internal and external support systems such as TRIO programs, career services, community agencies, and public and private foundations.

Hopefully this list of best practices will be helpful to other community colleges interested in implementing learning communities in their own developmental programs. MCC has found these basic components to be essential to support student success; however, the model can be modified to fit specific student demographics and institutional needs.

Conclusion

The AIM for Success program has been transformational in many ways. It has raised awareness of the importance and relevance of developmental education at the community college by demonstrating new ways to help students succeed. It has served as an anchor for curriculum reform in developmental education by providing insight into what helps underprepared students succeed in an academic setting. In addition, the learning community design has provided a new model for faculty and student services professionals to work together. Finally, AIM has inspired a collegewide discussion about the importance of interdisciplinary collaboration not only in developmental education, but also in a number of disciplines. This has led to the formation of additional learning communities for different populations of students, intended to achieve the same levels of student success as the AIM program.

The AIM for Success program can be adapted for other institutions. Its financial requirements are minimal, and a core group of existing faculty and staff are usually eager to participate. By incorporating the key components of administrative and faculty support, a shared philosophical framework, and solid guidelines and procedures, MCC's program can be tailored to fit into individual colleges' existing structures and processes.

AIM's supportive, nurturing atmosphere has helped many MCC students face multiple academic, social, and economic barriers, become comfortable with the learning process, and gain the skills and self-confidence they need to be successful throughout their educational journey. By applying the power of a learning community to the needs of developmental education students, colleges can fundamentally transform their instructional delivery, and ultimately, their students' success.

References

Boylan, H. R. *What Works: Research-Based Best Practices in Developmental Education.* Boone, N.C.: Continuous Quality Improvement Network with the National Center for Developmental Education, 2002.

Metropolitan Community College. "New Connections for Learning—Year Three Performance Indicators." Omaha, Nebr.: Metropolitan Community College, Office of Learning Design and Support, 2003.

Tinto, V. "Classrooms as Communities: Exploring the Educational Character of Student Persistence." *Journal of Higher Education,* 1997, 68(6), 599–623.

SUSAN RAFTERY is dean of learning design and support at Metropolitan Community College in Omaha, Nebraska.

7

This chapter explores the evolution of open admissions and developmental education at the City University of New York, and discusses how CUNY and, in particular, Bronx Community College have addressed the challenges presented by underprepared college freshmen.

The Evolution of Developmental Education at the City University of New York and Bronx Community College

Nancy Ritze

Colleges across the country, especially those that offer open admissions, are being challenged by entering students who are underprepared for college-level work. In addition, these colleges are increasingly being held accountable for the impact of their expenditures on student outcomes. This chapter illustrates how the City University of New York (CUNY) has addressed this challenge by creating a policy that maintains a delicate balance between open access, excellence, and accountability, and how Bronx Community College (BCC) has responded to these policies with effective practices.

Emergence of Open Admissions and Developmental Education at CUNY

In 1846, Townsend Harris, president of the New York City Board of Education, introduced the concept of an "open door" in postsecondary education, arguing, "Open the doors to all. Let the children of the rich and poor take their seats together and know of no distinction save that of industry, good conduct, and intellect" (City College of New York, 2002, n.p.). This sentiment inspired the establishment of City College in 1847, the oldest public higher education institution in New York City. By the 1930s, three other colleges had also been established under the overall jurisdiction of the Board of Higher Education.

By the mid-1950s, competition for admission to four-year colleges in New York City had grown so dramatically that only 38 percent of the 160,000 applicants were admitted to its existing public higher education institutions. In response to this demand, the first community colleges (then called two-year or junior colleges) were established. Staten Island Community College was the first public two-year college in the city; Bronx Community College was formally established in 1957. Currently, the CUNY system serves more than 450,000 students through a graduate school, medical school, law school, eleven four-year colleges, and six two-year colleges.

The initial vision for BCC was to provide a solid academic preparation for "students in the middle." Founding president Dr. Morris Meister said, "We are profoundly obligated to help each boy and girl become all that he is capable of being" (Rosenstock, 1999, p. 7). Meister built the college with a strong focus on liberal arts and general education in order to prepare students to successfully transfer to a senior college or gain a job in the workplace.

Initially, BCC did not have a formal remedial program, although special courses in English, speech, math, and physics were offered for students who needed extra help. In the early 1960s, BCC and other CUNY community colleges were administering skills placement tests in order to determine which students would take these special courses. By 1966, BCC required all incoming students to take reading, writing, and mathematics placement examinations. The English department developed "writing laboratory" and "reading laboratory" courses for students who did not perform well on the placement exams. The mathematics department developed remedial courses for students who scored low on the departmental diagnostic exam. In addition, tutoring services were provided for remedial students.

In 1968, in response to increased demands for greater access to CUNY, the Board of Higher Education approved a plan for providing a tuition-free college education to every high school graduate by 1975. After additional pressure, "open admissions" was actually implemented in 1970—whereby students with either an 80+ average or those in the top half of their graduating class were admitted to a senior college and all others would be admitted to a community college.

As this open admissions policy was implemented, community college enrollment increased dramatically. At BCC, enrollment rose from 8,865 in 1970 to more than 14,000 in 1975; more than 50 percent of BCC's incoming students needed at least one remedial course in reading, writing, or mathematics. As more and more academically unprepared students arrived at BCC, graduation rates declined and dropout rates increased. By the fall of 1976, the semester-to-semester attrition rate was 28 percent.

Implementation of the Freshman Skills Assessment Program

In 1976, the CUNY board of trustees voted to implement the CUNY skills assessment program, which required students to demonstrate basic skills proficiency before continuing in the upper division of the university. The motivation for the change in policy was to guarantee high academic standards while counteracting grade inflation (City University of New York, 1976).

The CUNY skills assessment program provided a university-wide testing protocol that included the administration of standard reading, writing, and mathematics placement tests for all entering students. At BCC, the skills assessment tests were used for multiple purposes: to measure initial course placement in reading, writing, ESL, and mathematics; to measure progress through remedial sequences; and to prepare students for transfer to the senior colleges.

Once students were assessed and placed, CUNY and BCC approached the challenge of addressing students' skill deficiencies in a variety of ways, including developing special programs and initiatives for students, creating faculty development programs, and providing supplemental education for underprepared students. During the 1980s, CUNY began to support remedial efforts in the colleges through grants distributed as part of its University Skills Immersion Program.

Bronx Community College (supported by CUNY and other grant funding) began to offer a number of programs to prepare students for college-level work. The Pre-Freshman Summer Program provided students with assistance in basic skills during the summer before their first semester at the college. The Freshman Initiative Program provided year-round intensive remedial instruction and academic and personal support for students who required remediation in all three skill areas. In addition, the Intersession Basic Skills Immersion Program offered midyear workshops (between semesters) for those students likely to pass the skills tests after an additional two or three weeks of intensive instruction. These early interventions and continuous reinforcements significantly accelerated rates of basic skills completion for participating students (Bronx Community College, 1994).

Developmental Education at CUNY Comes Under Attack

In the spring of 1997, Mayor Rudolph Guiliani and conservatives on the CUNY board of trustees publicly criticized CUNY, speaking out against the system's remedial policies, low academic standards, sub-par student performance, and low graduation rates. In addition, they vowed to "scrutinize standards and the university's remedial programs, which many of the students must take because they failed CUNY's placement exams in reading, writing, and mathematics" (Arenson, 1997, p. B3). The same year, the CUNY board of trustees passed a resolution that required community college students to pass a writing test in order to graduate or transfer to an upper-level institution.

In addition to these attacks, Mayor Guiliani commissioned an advisory task force to study and analyze the state and future of CUNY. The task force report, titled *The City University of New York: An Institution Adrift* (CUNY Task Force, 1999), presented the following critique of the university:

> Central to CUNY's historic mission is a commitment to provide broad access, but its students' high dropout rates and low graduation rates raise the question: "Access to what?" There is tragic personal loss and institutional waste implicit in CUNY's high dropout and low graduation rates. Moreover, the absence of clear standards of academic achievement tied to admissions and graduation permits doubts to fester about the value of CUNY degrees . . . CUNY must reinvigorate its commitment to excellence, while maintaining its commitment to providing broad access. (pp. 5–6)

The report concluded with a series of recommendations, including the following:

Reconcile access and excellence so that CUNY can provide the full range of postsecondary offerings from associate to graduate degrees while supporting broad access, high standards, and "top-tier" senior colleges.

Develop clear, objective standards for admission, readiness for college-level work, and graduation.

Rethink remediation and reinvent open admissions so that remediation occurs at the community college sector.

Modernize the student assessment testing program to ensure that tests measure skills appropriately for purposes of initial placement, progress, and certification.

Implement outcomes-based accountability at CUNY to encourage strategic planning and implementation, regular performance assessment, and development of incentives and rewards.

These recommendations presented CUNY with the challenge of maintaining open access, establishing high performance standards, and developing concrete systems of accountability.

CUNY's Systemic Response

To confront the challenge presented by the task force report, new standards for admission and certification were implemented at CUNY colleges and universities. The most significant change involved the elimination of remediation at the CUNY senior colleges, which was approved by the CUNY board of trustees in January 1999. The resolution stated: "Following a college's discontinuation of remediation, no student who has not passed all three Freshman Skills Assessment Tests, and any other admissions criteria which may exist, shall be allowed to enroll and/or transfer into that college's baccalaureate degree program" (City University of New York, n.d., p. 3). These dramatic changes followed almost two years of citywide controversy and contention, which continued to be argued in a variety of venues, including the courts and the press.

To ensure that students obtain the basic skills necessary for college-level work, the CUNY board of trustees approved required "exit from remediation" examinations for all students to ensure appropriate preparation for college-level courses. Finally, to ensure proper preparation for the upper division, the CUNY board of trustees also approved the establishment of a CUNY proficiency exam that would be required of all students in order to graduate from an associate degree program and for those who transfer to (or advance in) the upper division of a senior college (City University of New York, 1998).

CUNY's dramatic policy shift represents one response to the larger national debate over remediation. Questions about how best to address postsecondary students' skill deficiencies, where such remediation should occur, and who should provide financial support are being raised at the disciplinary, institutional, and state levels.

The presence of remedial education at the postsecondary level is extensive. In a recent study conducted by the National Center for Education Statistics, it is reported that in fall 2000, approximately three-quarters of institutions enrolling freshmen offered at least one remedial course. In that same year, more than one-quarter (28 percent) of entering freshmen were enrolled in at least one remedial course. Public two-year colleges were most likely to offer remediation (98 percent) and correspondingly had the largest proportion (42 percent) of freshmen enrolled in remediation (U.S. Department of Education, 2003).

Bailey (2003) suggests that community colleges will play an increasingly significant role in providing remedial education, because many students will remain unprepared for college-level work and institutions and states will move (as did CUNY) to require adequate preparation for entrance to the four-year institutions.

Roueche and Roueche (1999) argue that "what happens between the underprepared student and the postsecondary institution is of such importance that it has perpetuated a simmering controversy for at least three decades" (pp. 10–11). Indeed, state legislatures have become increasingly concerned about the costs of postsecondary remediation and about providing financial support for basic skills instruction at both the K–12 and postsecondary levels. The National Conference of State Legislatures (2001) reports a variation in state responses to this concern. Four states (Colorado, Florida, Texas, and West Virginia) have state laws requiring placement exams for entering freshmen; at least seven states have policies on how freshmen in public institutions of higher education are tested and placed. Four other states (Kansas, Montana, Nebraska, and North Dakota) have not set statewide policies on remediation.

Bronx Community College's Response

Despite the controversy brought on by CUNY's decision to move all remedial education to its community colleges, BCC welcomed the new admissions and certification standards. There was a sense of relief that students with remedial needs would still have access to the community colleges and that remediation would not be limited for those students.

Bronx Community College continues to serve one of the most diverse and at-risk student populations in CUNY, and indeed, across the nation. Almost one-half (47 percent) of BCC students report household incomes of less than $15,000 per year, one-third (31 percent) are single parents, most (96 percent) are ethnic minorities, about one-half (47 percent) are first-generation Americans, most are first-generation college students, and a great majority (88 percent) require remediation in at least one skill area. Thus, BCC's basic skill programs greatly contribute to its students' overall success. Given the clear skills proficiency standards that must be met by all students, BCC aims to maximize the efficiency of basic skill instruction. In doing so, BCC addresses the particular learning needs of each student and provides ongoing assessment, advisement, and interventions.

Building on the successful skills immersion programs initiated in the 1980s and the changes that came with CUNY's 1999 resolution, BCC now offers a wide variety of opportunities for students to develop the basic skills necessary for college-level coursework. These opportunities include precollege skills programs (ranging from summer immersion courses to semester-long programs), special freshman programs (that link remedial and content courses), basic skills workshops (offered between semesters), and tutoring and individualized instruction (in special labs or centers).

BCC Language Immersion Program (CLIP). CLIP is a one- to two-semester immersion program for college-bound students who have very limited English language proficiency. In this precollegiate, noncredit environment, which requires a small tuition payment, students can improve their English literacy and college preparation without jeopardizing their academic record or financial aid package. Since its inception in the summer of 1996, CLIP (which is housed on the BCC campus) has served 2,830 students, with approximately 275 enrolled each semester.

Pre-Freshman Summer Program. The Pre-Freshman Summer Program (supported by CUNY) provides free basic skills courses to more than a thousand incoming and continuing freshmen each summer. Pass rates in this program are higher than the regular semester rates. The program's benefits are particularly strong for incoming first-semester students; one-year retention rates for those who participated in the summer program are 80 percent, compared with the collegewide rate of 60 percent.

Freshman Initiative Program (FIP). In semester programs such as FIP, BCC places emphasis on mastery of one remedial subject for an intensive five-week period. FIP, which was originally developed with Title III funding and is now supported by CUNY, is designed for entering students with the lowest skill levels. FIP consists of one remedial course per five-week period, and is characterized by small class sizes, specially selected faculty, unique tutoring integrated into the classroom, individualized attention, and an early academic warning system. If students' remedial skills are mastered within the first five weeks, they move to the next skill level or a different basic skill area. If a skill is not mastered, students may continue in the same area until they can demonstrate competency. Pass rates in FIP courses are higher than the college averages. For example, in fall 2002, the remedial course pass rate for FIP writing was 70 percent (the college rate was 51 percent), for FIP reading it was 86 percent (the college rate was 66 percent), and for FIP math it was 82 percent (the college rate was 60 percent).

Basic Skills Workshops. In addition to offering special courses and programs, BCC offers many opportunities for students to participate in intensive workshops—during or between semesters—to build skills and demonstrate proficiency. Given the preponderance of skills assessment testing at all CUNY colleges, students usually complete a remedial intervention before they are tested. These interventions include regular remedial courses, workshops or intensive tutoring, or work with a skills center, such as the writing center or math lab.

Tutoring Programs. With significant support from a Title V grant, BCC has created and institutionalized state-of-the-art writing and math centers. The writing center was created to support both basic and more advanced writing skills in a variety of ways. The facility includes a computer lab for classes and workshops, a smaller room with computers for individual student work, and a tutoring and conference room. In its first two years, BCC students participated in more than nine thousand tutoring sessions and four thousand open lab visits. As well, over twelve thousand students attended in-class labs and over one thousand attended basic skills workshops.

At BCC, students are encouraged to move through the remedial requirements as quickly and efficiently as possible, but they must demonstrate proficiency before exiting. Efforts are made to encourage students who are not successful to try different approaches, such as remedial courses, workshops, and tutoring.

Characteristics of Success

As support programs for remedial students have evolved in the years preceding and following the 1999 CUNY resolution, three institutional trends have contributed to the success of BCC's remedial programs.

Institutionalizing Grant-Funded Programs. Many of the effective remediation initiatives at BCC (programs, centers, and curriculum redesign) were initially funded through external funds, including Title III, Title V, and CUNY grants. Many initiatives, such as the writing center, have been institutionalized and are now supported by college funds. Others continue to be funded by CUNY and are now a part of a comprehensive program, titled Comprehensive Undergraduate Education, which is designed to strengthen the undergraduate program across the CUNY system.

Strong Leadership. Another critical factor in the success of the remedial efforts at BCC is strong academic leadership, at both the college and the departmental levels. The English and the Reading departments make consistent efforts to communicate with faculty about the standards and measurements for successful remedial completion (including, but not limited to, testing requirements). This communication takes the form of newsletters, manuals, workshops, and even the use of departmental meeting time to discuss pedagogy.

A Focus on Faculty Development. Faculty interaction and development is a high priority at BCC, and it in turn serves to enhance student learning. Each year, the president awards faculty development grants for professional development initiatives. As well, a cornerstone of a recent Title V grant has been the creation of a Center for Teaching Excellence that includes an instructional technology lab to enable faculty to learn and practice alternative instructional methods and new instructional technologies. The center has relied upon BCC faculty leaders to integrate ongoing faculty development activities that occur in and between academic departments and to share and discuss teaching and learning strategies as well as innovative and effective practices.

Developmental Student Outcomes

Bronx Community College developmental programs can chart significant progress over the past several years. The one-year retention rates of first-time freshmen have steadily increased from 63 percent in fall 2000 to 66 percent in fall 2002. Six-year graduation rates have also increased steadily, from 22 percent in fall 1995 to 25 percent in fall 1997. These increases in retention and graduation are representative of increases in course passing rates (2 percent increase from 2001 to 2003), decreased course withdrawal rates (from 16 percent to 13 percent between 2001 and 2003), increased pass rates for the exit from remediation exams (with writing and reading rates above the CUNY community college average), and a decreased proportion of students on probation (from 25 to 24 percent between 2001 and 2003). In addition, BCC's transfer rate to senior colleges has been increasing, as have the first-semester GPAs and first-year retention rates of BCC transfer students. Most recently, the one-year retention rate of students who transferred to CUNY senior colleges was 82 percent, and their average first-semester GPA at the receiving institution was 2.52.

With further funding from CUNY, BCC will begin to implement an even more closely coordinated program, which will include all remedial and developmental programs as well as other student supports such as tutoring, faculty development initiatives (such as writing across the curriculum), general education initiatives, and ongoing assessment. The evolution of BCC's developmental education program should result in continued improvement in student learning and outcomes.

Although the original controversy in New York City over remediation, access, and standards caused concern among many of the CUNY constituents, it would appear that BCC has fared well under the new policies. Entering students continue to come from very diverse academic backgrounds and the majority continue to demonstrate basic skill deficiencies, yet the college is making good progress in improving student achievement and success.

References

Arenson, K. "To Graduate Sunday. CUNY Students Must Pass Test." *New York Times,* May 28, 1997, p. B3.

Bailey, T. R. "Community Colleges in the 21st Century: Challenges and Opportunities." *CCRC Brief,* 2003, *15,* 1–4.

Bronx Community College. *Periodic Review Report Submitted to the Commission on Higher Education.* Bronx, N.Y.: Bronx Community College, 1994.

City College of New York. "City College Founder Townsend Harris," 2002. http://www.ccny.cuny.edu/pr/history/founder.htm. Accessed Nov. 18, 2004.

City University of New York. "Recent Board Resolutions on Testing and Remediation." New York: City University of New York, n.d.

City University of New York. "Minutes of the Proceedings of the Board of Trustees, April 5, 1976." New York: City University of New York, 1976.

City University of New York. "Minutes of the Proceedings of the Board of Trustees, November 23, 1998." New York: City University of New York, 1998.

City University of New York. "Minutes of the Proceedings of the Board of Trustees, January 1999." New York: City University of New York, 1999.

CUNY Task Force. *The City University of New York: An Institution Adrift.* New York: City University of New York, 1999.

National Conference of State Legislatures. "Postsecondary Remedial Education." Washington, D.C.: National Conference of State Legislatures, 2001. http://www.ncsl.org/programs/educ/RemedEd.htm. Accessed Nov. 19, 2004.

Rosenstock, M. *Four Decades of Achievement.* Bronx: City University of New York, 1999.

Roueche, J. E., and Roueche, S. D. *High Stakes, High Performance: Making Remedial Education Work.* Washington, D.C.: Community College Press, 1999.

U.S. Department of Education, National Center for Education Statistics. *Remedial Education at Degree-Granting Postsecondary Institutions in Fall 2000: Statistical Analysis Report* (NCES 2004–010). Washington, D.C : U.S. Department of Education, 2003.

NANCY RITZE *is associate dean of institutional research and planning at Bronx Community College.*

8

Community colleges can strengthen their ability to provide academic support to both developmental and college-level students by offering traditional remedial programs with a complementary, centralized unit of student success and retention services.

A Comprehensive Approach to Developmental Education

Kathleen E. Quirk

Community college educators are likely to agree that the majority of students arrive at their doorsteps with room to grow, both academically and personally. National studies indicate that between 36 and 41 percent of first-time community college freshmen enroll in at least one developmental course. Yet at institutions where remediation is recommended but not required, the participation rate in developmental education programs might be as low as 10 percent. The cognitive, social, and emotional growth of the students who do not enroll in developmental courses is generally left to the individual efforts of faculty and staff across campus and the willingness of students to ask for help. Hudson Valley Community College (New York) has taken a more aggressive and comprehensive approach to student underpreparedness by creating a retention unit to assist students who are not being served by the traditional developmental education program.

History of Hudson Valley's Dual System of Academic Support

Hudson Valley Community College, part of the State University of New York system, was founded in 1953 and today serves twelve thousand students and employs five hundred full- and part-time faculty. As the second largest institution of higher learning in and around the capital city of Albany, Hudson Valley offers more than fifty degree and certificate programs through its four schools: business, engineering and industrial technologies, health sciences, and liberal arts and sciences.

NEW DIRECTIONS FOR COMMUNITY COLLEGES, no. 129, Spring 2005 © Wiley Periodicals, Inc.

In the early 1960s, the college created a loosely organized developmental education program that included noncredit courses and stand-alone reading, mathematics, and writing labs housed in academic departments. Students electing to take developmental courses (approximately 10 percent of the student body) were required to spend two additional hours per week in the labs, meeting one-on-one with a designated faculty member or working independently on drill-and-practice software programs. Faculty maintained progress charts for each student, and lab attendance was calculated into the developmental course grade. Between 50 and 60 percent of students who registered for developmental courses completed them, and each department maintained its own records of student attendance and progress.

In 1985, with the help of a three-year, $107,000 Vocational Education Act grant, the institution introduced a new approach to student support, and without disrupting the existing organizational model for developmental education, created several centralized support units to strengthen instructional support and retention services for all students. Today, Hudson Valley's developmental program can best be described as a dual system of academic support that encompasses both the traditional menu of developmental courses in reading, composition, mathematics, study skills, and English as a Second Language that are taught and managed in the academic departments, and a network of programs and activities offered or coordinated by the college's Instructional Support Services and Retention unit.

Hudson Valley's Traditional Developmental Education Program. In Hudson Valley's traditional developmental education program, department chairpersons are accountable for noncredit courses that support approximately thirteen hundred developmental students each year (approximately 11 percent of the total population). Students who test below college cutoffs in reading, writing, and mathematics must register for a minimum of one developmental course. In addition to these students, others voluntarily register for developmental courses in response to an academic adviser's recommendation and in order to improve in a specific skill or subject area. Students enrolled in the traditional developmental education program are also encouraged to take advantage of the institution's complementary system of instructional support and retention services.

Hudson Valley's Instructional Support Services and Retention Unit. To create a more comprehensive system of academic support services, the college initially established two new units: the Office of Testing, Advisement, and Academic Placement, and the centralized Learning Assistance Center (LAC). Placement testing staff were hired to select an instrument and create a program that welcomed students to the college, measured basic skills proficiency, and linked students with their academic departments for advisement. To create a centralized LAC, three faculty members were relocated from separate departmental learning labs, and two reading and study skills instructors were hired. The new LAC began to market its services to students with self-determined academic needs as well as those enrolled in developmental courses.

In 1995, the college tightened the link between skills assessment and academic support and combined the LAC and the Office of Testing, Advisement, and Academic Placement. Two years later, Hudson Valley's open access student computer labs were added to the expanding unit, and in 2001 assorted institutional retention efforts, such as an early warning system, a freshman experience course, and a volunteer call center, were incorporated. The broad functional unit was renamed Instructional Support Services and Retention (ISSR).

The benefits of centralizing these various institutional services were immediately evident. Placement testing personnel expanded their narrow roles as academic gatekeepers and began working as part of a college student success team. To use a medical metaphor, the LAC focused less on emergency room services for at-risk students and more on academic health maintenance programming, providing support services to all students from the beginning of their academic careers. The open-access computer labs changed their identity from student recreational areas to academic learning centers. The main benefit, however, was that program administrators were given the opportunity to actively participate in campus planning. Once it was linked to student retention, developmental education became acknowledged as part of the formula for achieving Hudson Valley's mission of providing "dynamic, student-centered, comprehensive, and accessible educational opportunities that address the diverse needs of the community" (Hudson Valley Community College, 2000, n.p.).

Today, the ISSR unit provides academic assistance to all students, regardless of their skill level. Approximately twenty-five hundred students make 11,500 visits to the LAC each semester, thousands of students work with faculty in the computer learning centers, and thousands more participate in retention programs, workshops, and in-class activities. Nineteen full-time and approximately forty part-time ISSR employees (faculty, professional tutors, and staff) stay abreast of best practices in academic support services, introduce new programming, and instigate, facilitate, and promote student success efforts across the campus. A yearly budget of approximately $800,000 (and regular vocational grant funding of up to $100,000) supports the unit's salaries and contractual expenses. In addition, academic departments and other student services offices often leverage their own resources to work collaboratively with the "retention folks."

Instructional Support Services and Retention Initiatives

To support students enrolled in developmental courses, academic advisers add unique course numbers to students' schedules that correspond to specific support services and activities. Although the instructional support activities are not graded and do not appear on students' transcripts, learning center contact information is listed on students' schedules, helping to remind them that they have been advised and have agreed to seek additional academic support. Learning center faculty then meet with students to establish an instructional support plan and a calendar of appointments throughout the semester.

Program Enhancement. Often, learner support initiatives take the form of enhancements to existing programs. Several Hudson Valley learning center workshops have been customized to serve students in freshman orientation courses. Students now attend one workshop on early recognition of academic problems and another that emphasizes the importance of time management, topics that learning center and orientation course instructors believe are crucial for first-semester success.

Faculty Collaboration. Although the learning center always worked closely with classroom faculty, the focus on student retention at Hudson Valley makes faculty collaboration even more important. Computer learning center specialists have begun to give classroom presentations and now develop and model lessons that incorporate basic software instruction (such as PowerPoint) into the directions for a specific class project. These lessons are developed jointly, and the classroom instructor is free to use them in subsequent semesters.

Another opportunity for modeling developmental education practices arises when learning strategies specialists arrange to go into classrooms to help students review for their first test and to provide tips for studying and test-taking. Most classroom instructors who have participated in this effort have subsequently added a test preparation lesson to their own syllabi. In addition, math specialists routinely visit first-semester math classes to talk about learning center services; they also distribute textbook stickers to remind students about instructional support services that are available to them when frustration sets in. Along these same lines, the learning centers recently obtained funding through the President's Innovation Fund to purchase sticky notes that refer students to the learning centers. Faculty affix these notes to students' papers when they feel additional help is necessary.

Peer Tutoring. Besides providing these services, the ISSR unit has created two variations on a standard peer-tutoring model to support students who might not seek help on their own. The first variation allows instructors to request a tutor to provide hands-on assistance during lab sessions. Instructors often suggest former students who are familiar with their individual instructional styles, and former students are often flattered by an instructor's request for help. A different option is offered when a qualified tutor for a high-risk course is unavailable. The instructor is asked to identify a current student who excels in the class. This student completes an abbreviated peer-tutor training session (through the learning center) and works with the instructor to arrange times to lead a study group before or after class. This program is popular among instructors who teach courses that require sequential learning; students receive help on a weekly basis from a classmate who was recently exposed to the same material in the same manner.

Another nontraditional tutoring effort, one designed to entice minority students to use tutoring services, is called Tutor Tuesdays. After meeting with minority student support staff to get their advice, learning center and Educational Opportunity Program (EOP) math specialists joined forces to offer tutoring in the more relaxed atmosphere of the campus center. Every Tuesday, approximately thirty minority students seek assistance with math and business coursework in this alternate location. On surveys administered at the end of the semester, students who have never visited the traditional learning center report that the tutoring "helped my understanding of the material" and "my grades are better as a result of the help I receive." The LAC has established a similar program in another campus building for the technology division this year.

Call Center. In addition to offering services through the learning centers, ISSR staff coordinate other learner support and retention efforts. For example, full-time college employees make evening calls to students at timely points during the academic year. Call center employees are paid an hourly rate to welcome students to the institution, urge them to schedule classes, remind them of registration dates and outstanding admissions documents, and inquire about problems. Because they have electronic access to student admissions and financial aid records, callers can immediately identify stumbling blocks for each student and propose solutions or send messages to appropriate departments for follow-up. Call scripts are easily customized to include messages for targeted groups, such as encouraging females in technology programs to join a campus support group. College enrollment data indicate that students have been completing their registration earlier for the past several years; in fall 2004, paid enrollment by the first week in August was up 24 percent from the prior year. Hudson Valley believes the calls are the reason for this change, and call records indicate that parents and students are extremely impressed by the institution's personal attention.

Support for GED Students. Another program component focuses on students without a high school diploma or GED, a high-risk population at Hudson Valley. In New York State, a student may be issued a New York State High School Equivalency Diploma upon successful completion of twenty-four college credits. This diploma allows students to become recognized candidates for college-level degree or certificate instruction at an approved institution. Students applying for this program meet with admissions counselors individually and take the college placement test to determine eligibility for enrollment. Enhanced student support, instigated by the ISSR unit, now includes a customized in-take form that is forwarded to the program's general studies adviser. The adviser, after meeting individually with students, shares information with the retention specialist, and a communication plan is put in place. The retention specialist calls students several times through-out the semester, checks in on their progress in developmental and credit courses, recommends specific learning center workshops, makes referrals to specific campus personnel, and reports back to the department adviser. Preliminary results indicate that the retention specialist is often able to detect problems and issues such as previously undisclosed learning disabilities and intervene before they become obstacles to student success.

Early Warning System. Another of Hudson Valley's retention pro-grams, an early warning system, is undergoing extensive refinement. In the past, the college mailed letters to at-risk students by the third week in the semester, and then to all students with midterm averages below 2.0. When distance learning faculty indicated that the third week was too late to sound an alarm for their students, the call center coordinator added a session to con-tact distance learning students who failed to log on or complete an assign-ment by the end of the first week of classes. Callers, who implemented the program enhancement this fall, were trained to assist students with technical difficulties and correct misconceptions about online learning.

Another learner support initiative related to early academic interven-tion was developed after a department chair expressed a concern that advis-ers were not able to spend enough time counseling students with poor midterm averages because they were busy scheduling students for the next semester. The midterm warning letter now refers students to the computer learning centers and an online survey that provides individualized recom-mendations for study strategies and referrals to institutional support ser-vices. Learning center faculty and staff have been trained to discuss survey results and offer suggestions for specific follow-up.

Campuswide Planning and Evaluation. In addition to the preceding programs and services, the associate dean of ISSR assembles campus work groups made up of personnel from academic and student services depart-ments to study and address other retention issues. One group just completed a review of campus services for students who identify themselves as unde-cided about a major, also a high-risk population at the college. As a result of the study, offices across campus are introducing institutional enhancements to services for undecided students, including a customized orientation event ("ropes" course activities), customized sections of the freshman orientation course (that include personal and career exploration activities), targeted invi-tations to career-related events (such as job fairs), and open house sessions for students who do not have clear academic goals and their parents (focus-ing on institutional career exploration and counseling services).

System and Budget Integration. With a centralized system and budget, ISSR administrators are also able to direct resources, both human and monetary, to student support services anywhere on campus. For example, the LAC assigned a part-time faculty mentor and tutor to help the athletic department raise the retention rates of student athletes. After designing an academic progress monitoring system and implementing an academic kickoff session for football players who begin the academic year with time-consuming team commitments, staff members reported an increase in participating athletes' GPAs from 2.02 in fall 2000 to an average of 2.32 in fall 2001, 2002, and 2003.

Supported by $9,000 in Perkins grant funding secured by the ISSR unit, the Center for Effective Teaching (CET) offers a faculty mentorship program to increase in-service training on the use of instructional technology in the classroom. Full- and part-time faculty made six hundred visits to the CET resource room during the fall 2003 semester and interacted with mentors who emphasized the pedagogical advantages of instructional technology and demonstrated state-of-the-art hardware and software. During 2004–05, an additional $9,000 in Perkins grant money is funding CET mentors who support particular groups of faculty, such as those teaching the freshman orientation course. Perkins funding also allows the learning centers to deploy part-time faculty to extend the hours that science labs and study centers are open. This provides increased access to specialized equipment that is not available to students in the learning centers. These kinds of initiatives are made possible though grant monies awarded for creative programming, academic support services, and a unit budget line for part-time instructional staff that can be allocated to enhance any campus program that provides direct service to students or faculty.

ISSR administrators also lobby for institutional change in other areas of the campus. Although they are not always successful (a push for a supplemental advisement center did not succeed), they are frequently sought out for advice. For example, a unit administrator on the planning committee for new faculty orientation recommended a greater emphasis on student success. As a result, information about the changing profile of the community college student and interactive teaching circles that focus on student engagement are now offered, in addition to welcome speeches by college, department, and union leadership; instructions for completing time sheets and submitting grades; and training provided by environmental health and safety staff.

Success Strategies

In 2000, Hudson Valley's comprehensive approach to developmental education was identified by the American Productivity and Quality Center and the Continuous Quality Improvement Network as an effective way to work with underprepared students. The college has been successful because its dual system of academic support excels in three main areas: program strategy, instructional approach, and learner support.

Program Strategy. The gradual but steady growth of Hudson Valley's developmental education program did not happen by chance; along the way, college and program administrators worked consistently to create a campus system for student support. They centralized small student support efforts and combined staff and budgets to make the best use of institutional resources. They hired faculty to provide instruction in the learning centers, giving these centers the status of an academic department. They created the position of associate dean to oversee the total operation and then added a full-time retention specialist.

Whereas many developmental education programs struggle for resources, and many dedicated faculty work in isolation to serve small numbers of students, Hudson Valley's integrated model makes significant institutional contributions. Faculty and staff workloads and schedules are developed with enough flexibility to allow them to engage in a variety of projects so that they are not restricted to a single service in the college. Unlike many developmental and learning center instructors who cannot leave their areas unattended during the school day, learning center faculty are encouraged to participate in campus meetings, investigate interesting programs at other institutions, and attend training sessions in the Center for Effective Teaching. Part-time professional tutors provide students with a high level of academic support, and full-time faculty interact with colleagues to identify student and faculty needs.

In addition, every nonteaching professional in the ISSR unit has campus outreach responsibilities. The placement testing coordinator trains new academic advisers and maintains the advising manual and Web site in addition to overseeing the ASSET and COMPASS placement testing program. The retention specialist coordinates the call center, a support program for students without a high school diploma, and the institutional early alert program. The unit's associate director maintains the online learning center, represents the unit on a distance learning team, and serves on a committee to design the faculty professional development program. The associate dean leads retention work groups, works on accreditation and mission-review committees, and serves on institutional communications and assessment committees. By design, all unit members interact with the campus at large and have firsthand knowledge of institutional needs, concerns, and plans. They are deliberately positioned to anticipate campus change and potential challenges, and to play active roles as campus problem solvers.

Instructional Approaches. In addition to having a clear strategy to positively affect the institution, Hudson Valley's developmental education program employs a wide variety of instructional methods and materials to meet the needs of its diverse population. Traditional developmental classes are limited to twenty students and are offered in a variety of settings to meet students' needs, including traditional classrooms, technology-equipped classrooms, and online.

In addition, the large, multifaceted ISSR unit has offices and learning centers located in several places on campus and provides access to any number of instructional environments. Faculty and staff meet with students one-on-one and in small groups, using blackboards, whiteboards, projection systems, handouts, worksheets, texts, and other media. To respond to the increasing number of students taking courses off-site, on the weekends, and through distance learning, the LAC created and maintains an online learning center that offers students informational material, short workshops, and instructional brush-up modules. Students also have access to specialized software in the institutional computing system, are given top-ten lists of instructional media maintained by the library, and can correspond with faculty and staff via e-mail.

Although assigned primarily to a single work location, faculty members interact with students at tables and computer workstations, in conference rooms, and in labs and study centers across the campus. They extend their instructional repertoire by teaming with other faculty and taking advantage of campus professional development opportunities.

Creative Learner Support. Providing creative learner support is essential for any developmental education program, and the comprehensive structure at Hudson Valley provides abundant opportunities for campus networking and staff brainstorming. Following the academic health maintenance model, ISSR staff consider every interaction between a student and the institution to be an opportunity for positive intervention. Unit members examine entering students' experiences and look for anything that might inadvertently reinforce their uncertainty about college study. New program ideas spring from observation of campus registration and midterm notification procedures, from data and information received at campus committee meetings, from the examination of student outcome measures, and from networking at conferences. Program conceptualization and design take place at monthly staff meetings, scheduled professional development sessions, and during sessions set aside for project development. In a centralized unit, one or two team members can be assigned to research and flesh out a program idea while others maintain the day-to-day obligations of the operation.

Conclusions

Hudson Valley Community College has created a comprehensive and extensive developmental education program that builds on the existing and effective system for delivering noncredit instruction and links discrete offices with related goals under a single banner of student success and retention. By all measures, Hudson Valley's dual system of academic support has been a wise institutional move; it not only prepares students with weak skills for postsecondary instruction but also provides supplemental academic intervention services for all students. Instructional Support Services and Retention administrators participate in the institution's strategic planning and assessment processes, and the institution's five-year academic plan now includes goals for student success and retention. Under the dual program model, developmental education at Hudson Valley Community College has been elevated to an institutional priority.

References

Hudson Valley Community College. "About Hudson Valley Community College." Troy, N.Y.: Hudson Valley Community College, 2000.

KATHLEEN E. QUIRK is associate dean for instructional support services and retention at Hudson Valley Community College.

*Four elements contribute to a classroom's success or
failure as a learning environment: student needs,
instructor approach, course content, and institutional
setting. This chapter discusses the challenge of aligning
these elements in the developmental classroom.*

Pedagogical Alignment and Curricular Consistency: The Challenges for Developmental Education

W. Norton Grubb, Rebecca D. Cox

Developmental education is not going away. Driven by increasing numbers
of students leaving high school underprepared and growing numbers of students whose first language is not English, developmental education may be
growing. When added to the "hidden" remediation that takes place when
instructors in college-level courses find their students unprepared (Grubb
and Associates, 1999), the extent of basic skills instruction in community
colleges is substantial.

Despite the evident need and recurring debates, there has not been sufficient or uniform progress in developmental education over the last few
decades. Some promising practices have emerged, particularly embedding
developmental education in learning communities (see Chapters Five and Six
in this volume), but these practices vary widely, few have become widespread,
and almost no evidence exists to confirm the superiority of one practice over
another. Dropout rates in remedial courses are high, student dissatisfaction
is high, and even students who complete developmental coursework do not
complete programs at the rates of their peers (Morris, 1994).

In this chapter we do not present simple solutions to these thorny problems. On the contrary, we initially complicate the issue by examining additional problems that have not been widely considered—particularly student
perceptions about what college and learning mean, the pedagogical alignment
between instructor and student, and the consistency of the overall developmental curriculum. By identifying these issues systematically, this chapter

provides a way of understanding why developmental education is often less effective than it could be, and suggests ways to improve its quality.

Overall, our analysis indicates that good teaching, in developmental education as elsewhere in the college, must be a collective process. The common situation where basic skills instructors teach in relative isolation from other faculty—in academic departments that offer little support for basic skills instruction and in colleges where administrators fail to coordinate resources—can never resolve the dilemmas of developmental education. Different approaches are necessary, some of which are outlined at the end of this chapter.

The Crucible of the Classroom: Contributions of the Instructor, Students, Curriculum, and the Institution

In every classroom, there are at least four elements that contribute to its success or failure as a learning environment (Cox, 2004; Lampert, 2001). Instructors, with different approaches to subject matter and pedagogy, are the most obvious. Students with differing levels of preparation and attitudes toward college and learning are the second obvious group. Curriculum or content is the third; sometimes it is shaped (at least in part) by the instructor, sometimes it is dictated by a textbook, and sometimes it is imposed from outside the classroom (for example, when a department uses a standardized curriculum, when the content of transfer classes is determined by universities, or when occupational instructors follow curricula established by industry associations, employers, or licensing requirements). Finally, the institutional setting also matters a great deal, because individual college practices, state funding and regulatory requirements, accrediting associations, and other external agencies exert powerful influences (Grubb and Associates, 1999).

When these four elements are in alignment with one another, classrooms are more likely to run smoothly and effectively. But potential problems arise whenever any of the four elements are out of equilibrium with the others. If, for example, instructors disagree with the curriculum, they may undermine or embellish it, sometimes for good and sometimes for bad. If institutions fail to support instructors, they undermine the faculty's ability to teach effectively. If teachers and students disagree about content or teaching methods, classes may become *distressed,* with evident tension between instructors and students, or may *collapse,* resulting in little learning taking place (Grubb and Associates, 1999). The particular problems that emerge depend on the specific details of how the four elements interact with one another, and they vary from class to class and from college to college. But problems are likely to arise whenever there is not equilibrium among the four.

The research literature offers substantive normative and how-to information about the attitudes of instructors toward students, subject matter, and their institutions. Our knowledge of institutional settings, and their consistency or inconsistency with efforts at instructional improvement, is also substantial, and certainly those working in community colleges know a great deal about local conditions. But our knowledge of students and their attitudes toward learning is sorely lacking, partly because empirical analyses of teaching usually focus on instructors rather than on students (Grubb and Associates, 1999; Hillocks, 1999; Richardson, Fisk, and Okun, 1983; Seidman, 1985). Similarly, the conventional descriptions of developmental students stress demographic characteristics (for example, first-generation college status and ethnicity) and external demands (such as employment and family), but aside from finding evidence of low self-esteem and external locus of control (Roueche and Roueche, 1999), there has been little effort to understand how developmental students think about their education.

Similarly, our understanding of how students move from initial assessments to developmental courses to college-level and advanced courses is also thin, particularly because coursework is often organized as a series of independent, instructor-dominated classes. Without confronting these inconsistencies and gaps in knowledge, the conventional questions about organizing developmental education and adopting "promising practices" are likely to lead nowhere.

Student Attitudes. Community college instructors know a great deal about students and their lives, and they are generally sympathetic to the "busied up" conditions caused by work and family responsibilities. However, instructors are much less likely to understand how students think about the purpose of college and the nature of learning. As Cox's research of composition classes in one community college (2004) and developmental writing courses at others (2001) reveals, students are highly *vocationalist:* they are virtually all using the college as a route to employment. As one student mentioned, "I want to get my Cisco certification . . . and then I could get a job and then get paid once I get my CCNA. And then I guess get a degree, like a bachelor's or something, and then get paid even more."

Similarly, a student in developmental writing explained his presence by saying, "I mean, you need to go to college; a high school diploma isn't going to get you the salary-paying job you need to support yourself." Vocational intentions in turn lead to highly instrumental conceptions of learning, embodied in the common question: "Why do I have to learn this?" Anything that is apparently unrelated to vocational goals—including developmental education—is systematically avoided; as one student asserted in reference to English and math, "There's a lot of stuff you don't use, so what's the point [of learning it]?" A great deal of academic content that matters to instructors is undermined by student perceptions of its irrelevance.

Surprisingly, given their vocationalist goals, students are often uncertain about their long-term careers (Grubb, 1996). As one explained, "I ain't sure if I want to be an EMT, nurse, lawyer—just whatever pays, so I can get out of debt." Often, they do not plan their courses and are ignorant about the educational requirements of occupations to which they aspire. Given these long-term uncertainties, students tend to focus on short-term and highly *credentialist* goals: earning the GPA necessary for passing courses (what Becker, Geer, and Hughes, 1995, labeled the 'GPA perspective"), earning credits for transfer, or completing a credential. One student noted the relationship between a professor's directives and the students' vocational goals: "I have to do what he tells us to do so I can pass the class, so I can get somewhere." Optimally, students would like to learn as much as possible as they pass courses and accumulate credits, but earning credits counts for more than the learning the credits are supposed to represent. Anything that seems unrelated to earning credits, or that requires extra work, is systematically devalued.

This attitude is exacerbated by an intense utilitarianism, as students weigh the costs and benefits of everything they do. If the effort (cost, time, or extra courses taken) outweighs the benefits (credits with vocational applicability), they will systematically avoid that effort, even if it might lead to more powerful learning. Students are concerned with "getting their money's worth" in every class, and about the potential for a "waste" of money or time. As one student noted, after finding out that she could have enrolled in a shorter certificate program, "I would just be taking those classes in that field. . . . I would have been able to go into the field, and then come back to school and take the stupid [core] classes later."

Consistently, students interviewed by Cox (2004) declared that college was *not fun*. In discussing her writing class, one student stated: "I think it is a necessary evil, pretty much. Because I don't know anybody that likes this class, but it's necessary if you want to be successful in your other classes. So I like the class on a learning standpoint. On a fun standpoint, I hate it."

In contrast to instructors who want students to be captivated by their subjects, students must depend on extrinsic, vocationalist, and often uncertain motivation to get them through their coursework. But the view that learning is *not fun* means that again students resist real learning and instead emphasize GPAs and credits. For example, rather than seeing revision as central to learning how to write, they expressed frustration because they want to "get over it." One student asked himself: "What's the least amount of change I need to make to get the paper accepted?" Another admitted making changes in response to instructor comments that she did not understand: "I just correct them, and I just get it over with, and get it accepted—'accept my paper and let's go.' That's it. That's the class. I don't care, as long as I pass it."

Most students seem to think that learning means accumulating factual and testable information. One noted that "Mr. Dobbs does put stuff on the board, and I appreciate that—that's like my enlightenment," but complained that he gives us "random essays that he finds." Students prefer "stuff on the board" and lectures as the most efficient way of learning, even though many instructors in community colleges avoid the lecture both as an inferior pedagogy and as an inappropriate relationship between teacher and student. Many students expressed real dislike of discussion ("don't waste my time for forty-five minutes") and complained that discussion-oriented instructors were "not teaching anything." One such student commented sarcastically at the beginning of a class, "Are we all ready for roundtable? Honestly, I feel like I'm back in high school—this is so stupid." She and other students interpreted the absence of lecture as an absence of instruction, and their understanding of professorial authority meant that any activities that transferred initiative to students—as in all student-centered pedagogical approaches—were rejected as "not teaching anything." So instructors who ask students to interpret reading rather than simply regurgitate facts, or who treat the social sciences as ways of understanding the world rather than a series of conclusions or *laws,* may find students resisting such instruction because they are *not learning.* In such cases, an observer can see students shutting down discussion rather than trying to develop their ideas; in response to one instructor's analysis of gender differences, two male students fended off discussion by saying: "Men and women are just different. It's like comparing apples and oranges." "Sometimes things can be simple. They don't always have to be complex." Many students in this class explained later that they were not there to hear from other students; they were there to get knowledge from the professor.

The most obvious problem is that many students systematically undermine their own learning. Students in these studies focused on grades rather than content, on efficiency rather than understanding, and on useful or *relevant* courses rather than those that might amplify their intellectual sophistication and afford some future, uncertain, and poorly understood benefit. And because schooling is *not fun*—partly because their previous schooling has often been relatively unsuccessful and sometimes demeaning—they are often fearful, scared of being caught unprepared, isolated, and intimidated by professors whom they view as distant authorities. A developmental student admitted, "I'm intimidated by hard stuff, so that's probably holding me back. I say 'that class is too hard,' instead of trying it out and applying myself." Such students' mechanisms of fear management are often counterproductive: keeping quiet in class, avoiding contact with the professor (so as not to "look like a fool"), avoiding "hard stuff" and classes with writing requirements, scaling down ambitions, failing to submit required work, and dropping out or stopping out.

Finally, students' views are inconsistent with what many instructors are trying to do, so there is a great deal of misalignment in classes. Indeed, students' counterproductive behavior often generates counterproductive reactions from instructors: shifting from discussion back to lecture and worksheets to control a class; retreating to facts and information transfer, because that is what students want; dismissing students as unprepared for college when they just need more encouragement; or expressing complete bafflement.

Of course, these students' views are not universal. As Cox (2004) observed, some students voice active dislike of lecture, understand that conceptual understanding is more important than factual acquisition, and are eager to participate more actively. In addition, students' attitudes about required courses, like writing and math, may differ from attitudes about elective courses and occupational coursework that seems "relevant." Our point is not that all students espouse counterproductive views, although we suspect that these attitudes are widespread. Rather, our interpretation is that student attitudes toward learning and the purpose of college are often unknown to instructors. The danger is that these views may be inconsistent with what instructors believe and detrimental to learning. Until instructors understand these attitudes, there may be disequilibrium in the classroom, missed opportunities, and in extreme situations, a complete collapse of content.

The most sophisticated instructors take care, particularly at the beginning of courses, to socialize students about their preferred pedagogy, but many more seem to assume that students know how to learn in different formats—seminar, lecture, workshops, or labs. In addition, students' experience of instruction can be distorted by the fears and low self-esteem they carry into the classroom. And finally, when different instructors have different conceptions of learning, students receive inconsistent messages, and—unless they are sophisticated in interpreting different pedagogical approaches—may spend much of their time bewildered by "what the instructor wants." In the conventional model of college, invisible disjunctions between students' and instructors' understandings become the *students'* responsibility. In a more collaborative model of teaching, part of the instructor's responsibility is to understand how students perceive college, the curriculum, and the nature of learning, and when necessary, revise their perceptions to facilitate learning. Changing students' attitudes may be difficult, because this process may mean having to fight against larger social trends and pressures including vocationalism itself, but it is more likely to be accomplished through collective action rather than by individual instructors.

Curricular Alignment. Collective action may also be required if a college's curriculum is to become aligned or consistent. This notion contradicts the practice of developing independent courses with different instructors (especially adjuncts) treated as interchangeable cogs in a wheel—a particular problem in developmental education with its high use of part-time instructors.

In the trajectory of developmental curricula, students are initially assigned or counseled into remediation based on their scores on an assessment test. Faculty often state that they do not know precisely what these tests measure, though they concede that "they do tell you something." Unfortunately, any testing procedure runs the risk of false assignment, where students are either unnecessarily assigned to developmental classes or placed into college-level courses when they do not possess the higher-level competencies they will need to succeed in these classes. Both types of errors lead to frustration for students and may reduce completion rates. In some colleges, developmental education has become voluntary for fear of incorrectly placing students into remedial classes. An added cost of putting unprepared students into regular classes may be the introduction of hidden remediation into college-level courses.

When students enter developmental courses, they are usually supposed to take one, two, or three courses, often in reading, writing, and math. Once students complete these courses, they move into college-level classes. If developmental courses are aligned with the demands of subsequent courses, all is well—assuming that the content of the courses is substantial, of course. But if the developmental courses are not coordinated with subsequent courses, students may exit developmental courses still underprepared. Some colleges have avoided this problem by creating special developmental courses for particular majors—math for nursing, for example. Others have created learning communities combining developmental English or math with introductory courses in health occupations, social services, or business. These approaches reflect collective rather than individual strategies to align developmental education with subsequent coursework.

Many colleges have adopted a roster of other developmental activities to bolster the effects of coursework, including learning labs, tutoring, counseling, and faculty development. In many colleges these activities have been created for different groups of students, such as older adults, English language learners, or welfare mothers. Yet it is unclear how these developmental activities are aligned with coursework (Perin and Charron, forthcoming).

Without some mechanism to coordinate all developmental courses and activities, there is no reason to think that developmental curricula and related activities will be aligned. What is wrong with the current structure is not entirely clear, because no one has done the institution-level research necessary to figure out how important each of the potential inconsistencies are, and few colleges have approached developmental education in a truly collaborative way. But we do know that students often view developmental courses as unwanted hindrances to their progress—the kind of education that seems useless or irrelevant to their vocational goals—and that they often fail to complete their developmental courses (Morris, 1994).

What Colleges Can Do: Developing Collective Approaches to the Classroom

Aligning the four elements of the classroom, in developmental education or in any other subject, requires much more than isolated instructors working with their own students. It involves considering many instructors' approaches to content and pedagogy, sequences of classes, students' prior experiences and attitudes toward learning, and the institutional requirements of improving instruction (including the need for resources). It may require working with (or perhaps against) the external requirements of state policies, accrediting agencies, and industry and employer groups. This is all too much to ask of any one instructor.

So the overall requirement for improving developmental education is not necessarily to look for specific practices like learning communities, even though that might be helpful, or to worry about organizational issues like mainstreamed versus centralized provision, and it is certainly not to search for some off-the-shelf curriculum or turnkey computer program because these usually foreclose faculty participation. Instead, the task is to develop a coherent plan for all elements of developmental education, to determine how the four elements of the learning environment can be coordinated—and *then* to determine the more specific policies that will improve developmental education. Developing such a plan might follow these steps:

Diagnose Student Perceptions. Community colleges should first begin the process of examining student attitudes toward college, toward their own learning, and toward developmental education. This may be one of the most challenging aspects of a coherent plan, because ethnographic interviewing, the common source of information about student views, is probably too time-consuming for most colleges. However, this information might also come from the collective experience of instructors, focus groups and individual interviews with students about their best and worst learning experiences, and more careful interviewing of incoming students about their motives for attending college. These data might indicate that some students—for example, those who are particularly hostile to academic work, and others who are particularly credential-oriented—might need developmental education in learning communities or internships so they can see how academic skills function in the workplace. Above all, instructors should inform themselves about the ways their students think about coursework and about college in general, and should operate—ideally, in unison—to dispel attitudes that are counterproductive. The use of counselors to diagnose student views strikes us as particularly valuable, because it could bring counselors and instructors together in a common cause.

Examine Faculty Perspectives and Support Faculty Learning. Diagnosing the attitudes of faculty—including adjuncts, who often teach most developmental courses—is also important. One purpose of this analysis is to weed out instructors who are hostile to underprepared students and to developmental education. A second, more supportive purpose is to create in-service programs to educate instructors about the roles of developmental education, about attitudes toward students, and about ways that teaching should be modified to consider—and in some cases to redirect—student attitudes toward learning. This would also remedy the problem of misdirected staff development in many community colleges, and it would help instructors learn about teaching through more than trial and error (Grubb and Associates, 1999).

Examine the Trajectory of the Developmental Curriculum. A third step, obviously necessary to achieve curricular coherence, is to examine the sequence of developmental activities: from initial assessments, to developmental courses, to college-level classes. Colleges should first ascertain the consistency among these elements, then improve the alignment of the different courses and other activities. This step requires the participation of both developmental and college-level faculty to make sure that developmental students are adequately prepared for the tasks required in college-level classes. If the courses are too varied—if, for example, the kind of writing required in literature, health, and business courses is unrelated—subject-specific developmental courses or learning communities might be required.

At this stage of planning, community colleges should consider the ancillary activities they provide to developmental students, often in an uncoordinated fashion. Each service should have a rationale, and a specific structure and organization. If, for example, students need tutoring in specific subjects, then individual departments may need to organize their own tutoring so it complements the courses they offer. If an identifiable group of students needs additional help getting through developmental education, then some kind of intensive learning may be necessary—but all-purpose learning labs or computer-based learning with drill-oriented programs might not be the right answer. If students have misconceptions about what will be required on the job, or what it takes to transfer, then internships, information sessions with employers or with students in four-year colleges, or mentorships may be necessary. A more coordinated or centralized approach to support services might prove to be more effective and efficient than the current pattern of distributed but uncoordinated services.

Assess Institutional Support. A fourth component of any coherent plan is institutional support for what occurs in the classroom. Unfortunately, many institutional influences are not particularly directed toward improving instruction, including the basic structure of the instructor's role, the amount of teaching required, hiring practices, promotion and tenure practices, pay scales and merit pay, preservice and in-service education requirements, the attitudes of administrators, campus culture, the relative underfunding of community colleges, and the neglect of student services (Grubb and Associates, 1999). The neglect of developmental education in many colleges is evidence that institutional support has been particularly scarce.

Colleges must begin with a clear-eyed diagnosis of institutional support, or the lack thereof, and clarify the necessary resources for improving different components of developmental education—including instructor time for collaboration, staff development, moral support from administrators, and additional funds for instructors. Obviously, obtaining extra funding in community colleges can be a difficult and politically charged task, particularly in times of scarce resources. But there is no point in pretending that developmental education will improve if institutional support is unavailable.

Develop an Overall Plan. The preceding four steps should cumulate into a coherent plan, one that specifies the elements necessary for curricular consistency, the requirements for effective instructors including pedagogical mastery and appropriate training, the ways of aligning students' attitudes with instructors' expectations, and the institutional support to make it all work. Such coherent plans have emerged in a few colleges. For example, a developmental studies department profiled by Grubb and Associates (1999) developed a *black book* of teaching principles, instructional materials, and workshops to prepare new instructors. Hudson Valley Community College (see Chapter Eight) has also developed a coherent plan. Unlike the hundreds of colleges in which developmental education is simply an accretion of practices emerging over time to respond to learning problems, these institutions have taken a step back to anticipate the issues their students present and to respond in coherent ways.

Developmental education in community colleges is one of the most difficult challenges our entire education system has to face. By this time in their education, students have often become demoralized, many have developed unhelpful attitudes toward schooling and learning, and most have increased work and family responsibilities that limit the time they have available for intensive study. Remedial approaches are necessarily second-best alternatives to reforming the way we educate students from their earliest days, and community colleges are forced to wrestle with problems not of their own making. But thankfully we do not (as many countries do) give up on these students. Facilitating equitable access to postsecondary education is, as the writers in this volume claim repeatedly, a central purpose of community colleges. Community college educators are committed to doing right by underprepared students, but this cannot happen until the full complexity of developmental education is recognized, and until colleges devote substantial resources to its resolution.

References

Becker, H., Geer, B., and Hughes, E. *Making the Grade: The Academic Side of College Life.* Chicago: University of Chicago Press, 1995.

Cox, R. D. "High School with Cigarettes: Negotiating Studenthood in a Community College English Class." Paper presented at the annual conference of the American Educational Research Association, Seattle, April 2001.

Cox, R. D. "Navigating Community College Demands: Contradictory Goals, Expectations, and Outcomes in Composition." Unpublished doctoral dissertation, School of Education, University of California, Berkeley, 2004.

Grubb, W. N. *Working in the Middle: Strengthening Education and Training for the Mid-Skilled Labor Force.* San Francisco: Jossey-Bass, 1996.

Grubb, W. N., and Associates. *Honored but Invisible: An Inside Look at Teaching in Community Colleges.* New York: Routledge, 1999.

Hillocks, G. *Ways of Thinking, Ways of Teaching.* New York: Teachers College Press, 1999.

Lampert, M. *Teaching Problems and the Problems of Teaching.* New Haven, Conn.: Yale University Press, 2001.

Morris, C. *Success of Students Who Needed and Completed College Preparatory Instruction* (Research Report no. 94–19R). Miami: Miami-Dade Community College, Institutional Research Office, 1994.

Perin, D., and Charron, K. "Lights Just Click On Every Day: Academic Preparedness and Remediation in Community Colleges." In T. R. Bailey and V. S. Morest (eds.), *Defending the Community College Equity Agenda*, forthcoming.

Richardson, R. C. Jr., Fisk, E. C., and Okun, M. A. *Literacy in the Open-Access College.* San Francisco: Jossey-Bass, 1983.

Roueche, J. E., and Roueche, S. D. *High Stakes, High Performance: Making Remedial Education Work.* Washington, D.C.: Community College Press, 1999.

Seidman, E. *In the Words of the Faculty: Perspectives on Improving Teaching and Educational Quality in Community Colleges.* San Francisco: Jossey-Bass, 1985.

W. NORTON GRUBB is the David Pierpont Gardner professor in higher education at the University of California, Berkeley.

REBECCA D. COX is a research associate at the Community College Research Center at Teacher's College, Columbia University.

Index

Back Issue/Subscription Order Form

Copy or detach and send to:
Jossey-Bass, A Wiley Imprint, 989 Market Street, San Francisco CA 94103-1741

Call or fax toll-free: Phone 888-378-2537 6:30AM – 3PM PST; Fax 888-481-2665

Back Issues: Please send me the following issues at $29 each
(Important: please include ISBN number with your order.)

_____

_____

_____

$ _____   Total for single issues

$ _____   SHIPPING CHARGES: SURFACE   Domestic Canadian
                                              First Item $5.00 $6.00
                                              Each Add'l Item $3.00 $1.50
                  For next-day and second-day delivery rates call the number listed above.

Subscriptions   Please __ start __ renew my subscription to *New Directions for
                  Community Colleges* for the year 2____at the following rate:

U.S.	__ Individual $80	__ Institutional $165
Canada	__ Individual $80	__ Institutional $165
All Others	__ Individual $104	__ Institutional $239
Online Subscription		__ Institutional $165

**For more information about online subscriptions visit
www.interscience.wiley.com**

$ _____   Total single issues and subscriptions (Add appropriate sales tax
                  for your state for single issue orders. No sales tax for U.S.
                  subscriptions. Canadian residents, add GST for subscriptions and
                  single issues.)

__Payment enclosed (U.S. check or money order only)
__VISA __ MC __ AmEx __ # _____Exp. Date _____

Signature _____ Day Phone _____
__ Bill Me (U.S. institutional orders only. Purchase order required.)

Purchase order # _____
                  Federal Tax ID13559302   GST 89102 8052

Name _____

Address _____

_____

Phone _____ E-mail _____

For more information about Jossey-Bass, visit our Web site at www.josseybass.com

authors discuss building community college foundations, cultivating relationships with the local community, generating new sources of revenue, fundraising from alumni, and the roles of boards, presidents, and trustees.
ISBN: 0-7879-7283-5

CC123   **Help Wanted: Preparing Community College Leaders in a New Century**
William E. Piland, David B. Wolf
This issue brings together various thoughtful perspectives on the nature of leading community colleges over the foreseeable future. Authors offer suggestions for specific programmatic actions that community colleges themselves can take to provide the quantity, quality, specializations, and diversity of leaders that are needed.
ISBN: 0-7879-7248-7

CC122   **Classification Systems for Two-Year Colleges**
Alexander C. McCormick, Rebecca D. Cox
This critically important volume advances the conversation among researchers and practitioners about possible approaches to classifying two-year colleges. After an introduction to the history, purpose. practice, and pitfalls of classifying colleges and universities. five different classification schemes are presented, followed by commentary by knowledgable respondents representing potential users of a classification system: community college associations, institutional leaders, and researchers. The final chapter applies the five proposed schemes to a sample of colleges for purposes of illustration.
ISBN: 0-7879-7171-5

CC121   **The Role of the Community College in Teacher Education**
Barbara K. Townsend, Jan M. Ignash
Illustrates the extent to which community colleges have become major players in teacher education, not only in the traditional way of providing the first two years of an undergraduate degree in teacher education but in more controversial ways such as offering associate and baccalaureate degrees in teacher education and providing alternative certification programs.
ISBN: 0-7879-6868-4

CC120   **Enhancing Community Colleges Through Professional Development**
Gordon E. Watts
Offers a much needed perspective on the expanding role of professional development in community colleges. Chapter authors provide descriptions of how their institutions have addressed issues through professional development, created institutional change, developed new delivery systems for professional development, reached beyond development just for faculty, and found new uses for traditional development activities.
ISBN: 0-7879-6330-5

CC119   **Developing Successful Partnerships with Business and the Community**
Mary S. Spangler
Demonstrates that there are many different approaches to community colleges' partnering with the private sector and that when partners are actively engaged in tailoring education, training, and learning to their students, everyone is the beneficiary.
ISBN: 0-7879-6321-9

CC118   **Community College Faculty: Characteristics, Practices, and Challenges**
Charles Outcalt
Offers multiple perspectives on the ways community college faculty fulfill
their complex professional roles. With data from national surveys, this
volume provides an overview of community college faculty, looks at their
primary teaching responsibility, and examines particular groups of
instructors, including part-timers, women, and people of color.
ISBN: 0-7879-6328-3

CC117   **Next Steps for the Community College**
Trudy H. Bers, Harriott D. Calhoun
Provides an overview of relevant literature and practice covering major
community college topics: transfer rates, vocational education, remedial
and developmental education, English as a second language education,
assessment of student learning, student services, faculty and staff, and
governance and policy. Includes a chapter discussing the categories,
types, and purposes of literature about community colleges and the
major publications germane to community college practitioners and
scholars.
ISBN: 0-7879-6289-9

CC116   **The Community College Role in Welfare to Work**
C. David Lisman
Provides examples of effective programs including a job placement program
meeting the needs of rural welfare recipients, short-term and advanced levels
of technical training, a call center program for customer service job training,
beneficial postsecondary training, collaborative programs for long-term
family economic self-sufficiency, and a family-based approach recognizing
the needs of welfare recipients and their families.
ISBN: 0-7879-5781-X

CC115   **The New Vocationalism in Community Colleges**
Debra D. Bragg
Analyzes the role of community college leaders in developing programs,
successful partnerships and collaboration with communities, work-based
learning, changes in perception of terminal education and transfer
education, changing instructional practices for changing student populations
and the integration of vocational education into the broader agenda of
American higher education.
ISBN: 0-7879-5780-1

CC114   **Transfer Students: Trends and Issues**
Frankie Santos Laanan
Evaluates recent research and policy discussions surrounding transfer
students, and summarizes three broad themes in transfer policy: research, student and academic issues, and institutional factors. Argues that
institutions are in a strategic position to provide students with programs for
rigorous academic training as well as opportunities to participate in formal
articulation agreements with senior institutions.
ISBN: 0-7879-5779-8

NEW DIRECTIONS FOR COMMUNITY COLLEGES
IS NOW AVAILABLE ONLINE AT WILEY INTERSCIENCE

What is Wiley InterScience?

Wiley InterScience is the dynamic online content service from John Wiley & Sons delivering the full text of over 300 leading scientific, technical, medical, and professional journals, plus major reference works, the acclaimed *Current Protocols* laboratory manuals, and even the full text of select Wiley print books online.

What are some special features of Wiley InterScience?

Wiley InterScience Alerts is a service that delivers table of contents via e-mail for any journal available on Wiley InterScience as soon as a new issue is published online.

Early View is Wiley's exclusive service presenting individual articles online as soon as they are ready, even before the release of the compiled print issue. These articles are complete, peer-reviewed, and citable.

CrossRef is the innovative multi-publisher reference linking system enabling readers to move seamlessly from a reference in a journal article to the cited publication, typically located on a different server and published by a different publisher.

How can I access Wiley InterScience?

Visit http://www.interscience.wiley.com

Guest Users can browse Wiley InterScience for unrestricted access to journal Tables of Contents and Article Abstracts, or use the powerful search engine.

Registered Users are provided with a *Personal Home Page* to store and manage customized alerts, searches, and links to favorite journals and articles. Additionally, Registered Users can view free Online Sample Issues and preview selected material from major reference works.

Licensed Customers are entitled to access full-text journal articles in PDF, with select journals also offering full-text HTML.

How do I become an Authorized User?

Authorized Users are individuals authorized by a paying Customer to have access to the journals in Wiley InterScience. For example, a university that subscribes to Wiley journals is considered to be the Customer. Faculty, staff and students authorized by the university to have access to those journals in Wiley InterScience are Authorized Users. Users should contact their Library for information on which journals they have access to in Wiley InterScience.

ASK YOUR INSTITUTION ABOUT WILEY INTERSCIENCE TODAY!